Puppy Love

Liz Palika, CPDT, CABC
Sheri Wachtstetter, Photo Editor

WILEY
Wiley Publishing, Inc.

Copyright © 2009 by Wiley Publishing, Inc., Hoboken, New Jersey. All rights reserved.

Howell Book House
Published by Wiley Publishing, Inc., Hoboken, New Jersey

For general information on our other products and services or to obtain technical support please contact our Customer Care Department within the U.S. at (800) 762-2974, outside the U.S. at (317) 572-3993 or fax (317) 572-4002.

Wiley also publishes its books in a variety of electronic formats. Some content that appears in print may not be available in electronic books. For more information about Wiley products, please visit our web site at www.wiley.com.

Library of Congress Cataloging-in-Publication Data:
Palika, Liz, 1954–
        Puppy love / Liz Palika.
                        p.   cm.
                Includes index.
                ISBN-13: 978-0-470-39317-8
                ISBN-10: 0-470-39317-3
                1. Puppies.   I. Title.
                SF427.P178   2009
                636.7'07–dc22
                                                                    2008046679
Printed in China

10   9   8   7   6   5   4   3   2   1

Book design by Erin Zeltner, with Tai Blanche
Book production by Wiley Publishing, Inc. Composition Services

Acknowledgments

Creating a book requires the help of many people, all of who deserve a great deal of thanks.

Although I have been training puppies and their owners for many years, in writing this book I also leaned on the expertise of my good friends, Petra Burke and Kate Abbott, of Kindred Spirits Dog Training in Vista, California.

Sheri and Buddy Wachtstetter are both talented photographers and expert photo editors. We have worked together on several books and I have always been pleased with their efforts. Several other photographers also worked with us, including Mary Fish Arango, Jean Fogle, and Melinda Peters, as well as several breeders who shared photos of their precious puppies with us. Thank you all.

Behind the scenes, many people are a part of creating a book. Thanks go to my agent, Marilyn, and my editors, Pam and Carol. Thanks, everyone!

Table of Contents

About the Author

Liz Palika has been writing professionally since 1985, when she was first published in *Dog Fancy* magazine. Since then she has written more than 60 books, more than 1,000 magazine and Internet articles and columns, and has provided expert advice many times, including for *Animal Planet Radio* and *Good Morning, America.*

One of her most recently published books is *The Howell Book of Dogs,* which won Best Reference Book in the annual Dog Writers' Association of America contest, and was also nominated for Best Nonfiction Book from San Diego Book Writers, Inc. For more on Liz's work, go to www.lizpalika.com.

Liz is a Certified Pet Dog Trainer (CPDT) and Certified Animal Behavior Consultant (CABC), and has been training dogs and teaching dog owners for more than twenty-five years. Although she has trained at all levels, from puppy through advanced obedience, her primary focus is pet dogs. Her goal is to help pet owners have a well-behaved family companion that will spend his life with his family. For more on Liz's training, go to www.kindredspiritsk9.com.

Introduction

A puppy is unlimited potential. With a little help from you, he can achieve anything. He may be your jogging partner, or he might scare away the monsters hiding under your child's bed. He may be a performance-sports star, a therapy-dog extraordinaire, or a dedicated service dog. Better yet, he may grow up to be your best friend.

You can find a new puppy in various ways. By adopting a puppy from a shelter, you could potentially save that puppy's life. Sometimes entire litters of puppies are brought to shelters because the owner of the mother dog couldn't find homes for the puppies. Although you may not know anything about this puppy's background (heritage, genetics, or sometimes even breed or mixture of breeds), you will feel wonderful knowing that you saved this small life.

A reputable breeder, one who is knowledgeable of her breed, is a great place to get a puppy, too. She will perform health tests on the father and mother of the litter in hopes of producing the healthiest puppies possible. You can also contact the breeder if you have any questions after you bring your puppy home.

Puppies also appear in people's lives unexpectedly. Perhaps a friend's dog has had puppies and your friend hands you a small, fuzzy soul with bright eyes. Riker, my now 9-year-old Australian Shepherd, joined our household that way. My husband and I weren't looking for a puppy; we had just lost a treasured dog and were still grieving. However, a good friend handed us this black, white, and copper Aussie puppy and said, "He hasn't found a home yet." After a lick on the face from that adorable puppy, what could we do? He was wonderful medicine for us then and still is today.

Choosing Your Puppy Wisely

Although Riker joined our household unexpectedly, he was of the breed that my husband and I have owned for years, Australian Shepherds. Because we know the breed well, we know the breed is a good fit for us. Aussies are very bright and need a lot of training and we can do that. They are very active and need daily exercise and we can meet those needs, too. Aussies also shed a lot; I have a good vacuum cleaner and hairy dust bunnies don't bother me!

Choosing the right breed is very important. Dog trainers see lots of dogs and owners that are a bad fit for each other all the time. A sedentary owner and a very busy, active dog are going to drive each other nuts. The owner will want to relax while the dog wants to do something, anything, now!

Other bad fits include:

- Small, fragile breeds, especially toy breeds, in households with busy, active, rowdy kids who want to play rough with their dog.
- Owners living in neighborhoods where loud-barking breeds can be heard easily by neighbors.
- Elderly owners who get puppies of breeds that are rough, overly playful, and slow to mature.

For the best match possible, do some research before adding a puppy to your household. Choose a breed (or mixture of breeds) that has characteristics that will complement you and your family, your activity level, your lifestyle, and your personality. My favorite book for this type of research is, of course, my book, *The Howell Book of Dogs* (Wiley, 2007), which profiles more than 300 breeds and varieties.

In This Book

In this book, I help you discover puppyhood in all its wonders, from birth to adolescence. In the first chapter, I look at the relationship your puppy has with his mother and littermates, what he learns from them, and how this applies to his relationship with you later.

Chapter 2 will help you prepare for your new family member's arrival while chapter 3 will start you on housetraining. This training is very important, obviously, and should begin as soon as you bring your puppy home. Chapter 4 discusses household rules and will help you decide what rules are important to you. For example, do you want to allow your puppy up on the living-room sofa?

Chapter 5 explains what the human-animal bond is and why it makes having a dog so special. In chapter 6, I talk about the importance of playing with your puppy, what games you can play, and which games to avoid.

Chapter 7 explains socialization and leads you through the process while chapter 8 helps you begin your puppy's training. In chapter 9, I discuss potential problem behaviors, how to prevent them from happening, and what to do should your puppy get into trouble. In chapter 10, I talk about caring for your puppy, from vaccinations through grooming. And in chapter 11, you learn what adolescence is all about and how to live through it.

Whew! When I say this book is all about puppies, I mean it. So read the book, mark the pages that are important to you, enjoy the wonderful photography, and then as your puppy grows and changes, come back to the book. Use it as a reference; that's why I wrote it for you. Hug your puppy for me and enjoy the book!

Liz

Golden Retrievers, 6 weeks old

Chapter 1

Welcome to the World of Puppies

Pugs, adult and 2-week-old puppy

Genetics Determine Your Puppy's Health and Temperament

No other species has been as welcome in our lives and homes as dogs. Although we have wonderful relationships with several domesticated species, including cats and horses, none of them participate in our lives as fully as dogs do.

The dog that your puppy will grow up to become is the result of nature (his heritage) and nurture (the care he receives and the experiences he faces when he joins your home).

The physical characteristics of your puppy's parents combine to create the appearance he will have as an adult dog. These include his height, weight, body shape, ear type, eye color, coat length, and coat color. If your puppy's mother and father are both of the same breed, then your puppy will share the characteristics of that breed. However, if the parents are of different breeds or are mixed breeds themselves, then your puppy may be quite unique, possessing attributes from each parent.

Your puppy's parents also affect his health. If his parents are physically healthy, then chances are he will be also. Genetic health is also important. Ideally, your puppy's parents should not carry any genetic problems or the tendency to develop health problems later.

Much of a puppy's temperament is derived from his experiences, but his parents' personalities play a role in determining his adult personality. If Mom and Dad are protective, the puppy will likely have that tendency, too. If the parents are sweet, affectionate, and loving, the puppy is apt to share those characteristics.

The parents also share their inherited "working" tendencies with their offspring. Dogs that herd livestock will share those working traits with their puppies, as will dogs who use their scenting abilities to follow game. Dogs who enjoy training and performance sports are more likely to produce offspring who are also easily trained.

Jack Russell Terrier, 9 days old

Puppy Development during the First Two Weeks

A female dog's pregnancy lasts from sixty to sixty-four days, and she can suffer from morning sickness, loss of appetite, and, during the later stages of pregnancy, general discomfort. When the puppies are born, they are blind and deaf, round and fat, and helpless. When born they have hair, tiny little toenails, and can already twitch their tiny tails.

During the first few days, a puppy is attracted to his mother's body heat because he cannot control his own body temperature. This attraction to heat enables him to find his mother and his sense of smell helps him find a nipple so that he can nurse. Because all of his littermates share this need for warmth, the puppies will cuddle together in a big pile to keep each other warm when the mother dog leaves to eat or go outside to relieve herself.

> **A puppy spends the vast majority of his first two weeks sleeping.**

At this age, puppies cannot walk; they move by making swimming motions with their legs. These motions also occur while the puppy is sleeping. Called *active sleeping,* these motions, along with muscle twitches, strengthen the puppy's muscles.

The mother dog must also help the puppy relieve himself. After the puppy has eaten, Mom will lick the puppy's belly and genitals to stimulate him to relieve himself. Then Mom will clean up after him.

A puppy spends the vast majority of his first two weeks sleeping. The puppy will nurse, get cleaned up by his mom, and then pile up with his littermates to sleep some more. And he'll repeat the whole sequence in a couple of hours. As he's doing this, though, he's growing rapidly and his muscles are getting stronger.

Puppies Grow and Change during the Third and Fourth Weeks

Many changes take place during the third and fourth weeks after birth. Although he's still sleeping a lot, a puppy is gradually snoozing less and becoming more aware of the world around him.

A puppy's senses change dramatically during these two weeks. His sense of smell gets better and he'll begin twitching his nose as he inhales odors. His eyes open, and within days the puppy will begin to track movements that happen in front of him. His hearing improves, too, and by the end of the third week he may even startle a little at sharp or unexpected sounds. As his senses develop, the puppy begins to recognize his littermates, his mother, and the people who care for him.

The puppy is also getting stronger and one day he will try to coordinate all four legs so that he can stand up. Once he's up, he begins walking. Although he's very unsteady, he gradually gets better at it.

His curiosity kicks in now, too, and he will begin exploring his surroundings. He and his littermates need a safe place because he has no common sense and could get lost or stuck in a bad situation during his explorations.

The puppy is still nursing strongly and is growing rapidly. Although his mom is still cleaning him, he is more able to relieve himself on his own and may begin toddling away from his bed to do so.

By the fourth week, all the puppies in the litter will begin playing. This is great fun to watch because the puppies are so clumsy and uncoordinated. But they have fun, try to wrestle, and even begin to bark as they play.

Border Collie, 3 weeks old

Border Collie, 6 weeks old

Puppies Become Toddlers in the Fifth and Sixth Weeks

A puppy is developing, growing, and changing rapidly during weeks five and six. He's changing from a baby to a toddler.

He's aware of his senses and is learning to use them. He can recognize his mother's and his littermate's smells, appearances, and the sounds they make. He also recognizes familiar people.

The breeder has been handling the puppy since birth, examining him to ensure there are no health problems and to make sure the puppy is gaining weight. But now the breeder will have other family members begin handling the puppy, too, so that he becomes accustomed to different people. He needs to get used to a variety of people in the next few weeks and months, but this should begin very gently and carefully so that the puppy is not frightened.

The puppy also becomes more aware of what is happening around him in the house, and that includes the sound of a vacuum cleaner, the sight and sound of a flapping trash bag, the sounds of music and television, and all the other sights, sounds, and smells of a home.

His mother will begin to wean him, and the breeder will introduce soft foods into his diet. Learning to eat these new foods will be a challenge, though, because he will initially try to suck them as if he were nursing his mother. But he will teach himself to eat through trial and error.

Even though he's weaned at this point, he needs to remain with his mom and littermates. At this age, they are vital in teaching him how to be a dog: how to play, how to get along with others, and how to accept limits on his behavior. Puppies sent to new homes during this important stage of development often have behavior problems later.

> 66 The puppy becomes more aware of what is happening around him in the house. 99

The Joys and Lessons in Play

During the fourth through sixth weeks of life, puppies begin playing in earnest. They wrestle with each other, roll around in a big puppy pile, and begin chasing each other as their legs get stronger.

As the puppies play, their muscles and bones get stronger. The puppies also gain coordination as they use their legs more. They learn to walk, then run, and then bounce and even jump. Granted, they only jump an inch or so initially, but they're learning how.

Toys become interesting during this stage, too, and puppies will use anything from a ball to an empty cardboard box as a toy. The puppy will investigate the object, shove it with his nose, paw at it with a front paw, and then try to chew on it.

Play is fun and great exercise for growing puppies, but it's also a learning exercise. The puppies who investigate strange objects are being socialized to strange things as they play and this is good for them. Wise breeders put a variety of different objects in with the puppies for this very reason.

As the puppies play more, breed differences also become evident. Border Collie puppies begin to stare with their eyes to initiate play just as they will stare at sheep when they herd them as adult dogs. An Australian Shepherd tends to play by knocking the other dog with his hip, potentially knocking the other dog off his feet, and Aussie puppies begin doing this early. Boxers play by "boxing" with their front paws. Many terriers like to hide in small spaces and then pounce on an unsuspecting littermate. It's fun to watch these traits develop.

Rottweilers, 4 weeks old

Labrador Retrievers, 16 days old

Littermates Teach Social Skills

As they play with each other, puppies also learn how to get along with each other. The social skills taught now will be with a puppy for the rest of his life and will have a bearing on his relationships with other dogs as well as with people.

As puppies wrestle and play, they learn their own strength, especially the power in their little jaws. If a puppy bites too hard during play, his littermate will yelp. If the biter backs off and gives his hurt littermate a lick of appeasement, then all is well and he is forgiven. However, if he continues to play too hard, his littermate will stop playing with him. Because his littermates are vital to him for both comfort and companionship, being shunned is a horrible experience for a puppy and a very effective means of helping him correct his behavior problems.

Dogs are experts at communication through verbal sounds, facial expressions, and body language. Puppies finely tune these skills during puppy play. For example, one puppy may initiate play by lowering his front end and leaving his hips standing up, at the same time wagging his tail. This posture, called a *play bow,* is an invitation to play.

Puppies also invite play with toys. One puppy might pick up a toy, shake it in front of a littermate, and growl. When one of his littermates grabs the toy, a game of tug of war or keep-away is on.

The breeder shouldn't interfere in puppy playtime even if play gets a little rough. The puppies can teach each other so much during this stage of development, more than we can ever understand, and our interference can have lasting repercussions. The mother dog is the best referee, and she will step in when things get out of hand.

Puppies Become More Independent in the Seventh and Eighth Weeks

A puppy's mother and littermates are still very important during the seventh and eighth weeks of his life. Although the puppy is weaned and no longer nursing, his mom still provides comfort and security and is teaching him the rules of being a dog. His littermates provide companionship and are the best playmates he could have. In addition, as he interacts with both his mother and his littermates, his communication skills continue to improve.

The puppies are playing more and although play often gets a little rough, that's OK. The puppies will teach each other and police themselves. As they gain coordination, they take turns chasing and tackling one another, all the while gaining strength.

Curiosity is well developed now, so puppies can potentially get into all kinds of trouble. They will sniff, paw, and chew on everything within reach. That means you must supervise the puppies or restrain them in an escape-proof pen. Puppyproofing the house and yard is also very important; put away anything the puppies could get into and potentially destroy or that could harm them. (See "Puppyproofing Your Home," later in this chapter.)

If the backyard has a safe place for puppies, they can go outside in good weather. Offer them safe things to explore and climb on, such as a cardboard box, a wooden plank, a concrete block, a big ball, some safe dog toys, and even a fireplace log.

Although many breeders send puppies on to their new homes at this age, many experts recommend waiting. In fact, many breeders have no problem holding on to puppies until they are 9 to 10 weeks of age because they are a little bigger and more confident at this age, and they settle in to their new homes with less worry.

Rottweiler, 7 weeks old

Golden Retrievers, 2-year-old adult and 9-week-old puppy

Momma Dog Is the Best Teacher

Your puppy's first and best teacher is his mother. Although puppies learn a lot from each other, a puppy and his littermates are excitable and emotional. However, a mother dog's maturity and natural maternal instincts make her lessons much more valuable to the puppy.

A good mom is caring and affectionate with her puppies. She protects them from danger and comes running when she hears them cry, but as they get older she also allows them a little more leeway to roughhouse and play. She will interfere, though, if things get too rough.

The mother dog also encourages play by holding a toy down in front of a puppy and shaking it slightly so the puppy grabs the toy. Mom will then simply hold on to the toy, allowing the puppy to pit his tiny strength against hers. Puppies learn many life lessons from play—more than we can comprehend—and Mom helps her puppies learn by encouraging them to play.

> "A good momma dog also teaches her puppies how to accept discipline."

A good momma dog also teaches her puppies how to accept discipline. When a puppy misbehaves, the momma dog corrects the puppy firmly and quickly (using a growl, snarl, or bark) and with just enough force (pinning the puppy to the ground) to stop the undesirable behavior. She never holds a grudge, she doesn't wander around for ten minutes muttering about the bad puppy, and she never hurts or scares the puppy. Nor does she give the puppy a choice; the puppy will accept the discipline. Not only is the momma dog a good example for you to follow as the puppy's new owner—caring; affectionate; fair, yet firm—but this lesson from momma dog makes it possible for you to teach your new puppy later.

Lots of Changes during Weeks Nine and Ten

Between 9 and 10 weeks of age a puppy grows rapidly and changes quickly. He becomes more independent and is more likely to wander away from his littermates rather than stay close to them. He explores as much as he can and gets braver about trying new things. Keeping him safe from himself is definitely more of a challenge now.

He is ready to go to his new home now and, when handled gently, will make the transition with little worry or fear. This is the age when puppies are able to bond with people, so you need to spend lots of time with him when he first goes home. Play with him, introduce him to a comb and brush, and snuggle with him.

A puppy is also more developed physically and can begin housetraining. Although he cannot hold his bowels and bladder for long, he is beginning to develop control. By starting housetraining now, you can prevent him from learning bad habits. You can introduce a crate to him and begin taking him outside with you to the place where you want him to relieve himself. (See chapter 3 for more on housetraining.)

Puppies at this age often use their mouths on people as they did with their littermates. However, the other puppies had a thick coat of hair and people do not! Plus, those puppy teeth are very sharp. A puppy needs to learn not to bite, but frequent corrections from you will often cause the puppy to fight back. So prevent the puppy from biting as much as possible (see chapter 9 for specifics), and then if he does, tell him, "Ouch!" Stop him from biting and then distract him by handing him a toy that he can play rough with as much as he wants.

Shih Tzu, 10 weeks old

Miniature Dachshund–English Cocker Spaniel mix, 7 weeks old

The World Is a Scary Place

Puppies are, for the most part, carefree and happy. However, the world occasionally appears frightening. A sudden sound or sight may startle your puppy, or he may notice something different that he hadn't paid attention to previously.

Kody, a Newfoundland puppy, walked out of his owner's back door one day and began barking furiously at the patio table. It had been there for longer than he had been alive, yet he apparently hadn't noticed it and thought it was quite scary.

Puppies are most prone to fear at specific ages, including 8 weeks of age and during teething between 4 and 5 months of age. However, every puppy is an individual; some go through these specific fear periods and others do not. Some get worried about things at 12 or 13 weeks of age. The age is not as important as your ability to recognize that your puppy is going though this developmental stage. And then you must handle his fears correctly so that he doesn't grow up to be a worried dog; you want a confident, curious puppy.

Kody's owner, Joan Swanson Hamilton, walked her puppy to the picnic table by encouraging him in a happy (not reassuring) tone of voice and saying, "Come on, you silly boy! It's just the patio table!" She then touched the table and chairs and encouraged him to approach them, too. When he did, she walked him away while continuing to talk silly to him.

If she had tried to reassure Kody, he might have misunderstood her and continued to think that the table was scary. By using a happy tone of voice, she conveyed the idea to her puppy that his fears were silly. Kody learned another important lesson, too, though. He learned to trust his owner's judgment.

The Best Age to Bring Home a Puppy

Most momma dogs stop nursing their puppies between 5 and 6 weeks of age. Although some moms continue feeding the puppies for a week or two after that, the momma's milk will dry up soon after the puppies begin eating solid food.

However, that doesn't mean puppies should leave their mom and littermates at this early age. When puppies do not have time to play, wrestle, and otherwise interact with their littermates, they lose valuable learning opportunities that will affect their behavior with both people and other dogs as they grow up. The lessons momma dog teaches are even more important, especially in regard to learning social behavior and accepting discipline.

The most common age for a puppy to go to his new home is 8 weeks of age. However, the drawback to getting a puppy at this age is the possibility of a fear period. If the puppy goes home with you and is worried about life, then he may develop carsickness (because the car took him away from his mom), he may worry about children (if your kids greet him while he's afraid), and he will be afraid of the veterinarian's office if he goes in the next day for vaccinations.

> "The best age to bring home a puppy is between 9 and 10 weeks of age."

Before bringing your puppy home, talk to your puppy's breeder about the right age to do this. If the puppy is bold and confident, then go ahead and bring him home. But if he's at all worried or cautious, tell the breeder you will pick him up the following week.

All things considered, the best age to bring a puppy home is between 9 and 10 weeks of age. He's probably past the 8-week-old fear period, he's had lots of time with his littermates and mom, and he's in the right stage of life to bond with people—specifically, you!

Labrador Retrievers, 9 weeks old

West Highland White Terrier, 11 weeks old

A Shopping List for Your New Puppy

You are going to need some supplies for your new puppy. Here is a basic list:

- **Baby gates.** Gates limit your puppy's freedom so he doesn't get into trouble. Buy enough that you can close off hallways and keep him in one room with you.

- **Cleaning supplies.** Puppies have accidents and track in dirt from outside. Enzymatic cleaners (available at pet-supply stores) are awesome for cleaning up housetraining accidents.

- **Collar and leash.** Choose a soft, buckle-type collar and a four- to six-foot leash that's comfortable in your hands.

- **Crate.** I talk about appropriate crate size for your puppy as well as crate training in chapter 3.

- **Food.** Pick up some of the food your puppy is used to eating. If you want to change it later, you can do so gradually.

- **Food and water bowls.** Unspillable ones are best!

- **Grooming supplies.** Pick up a shampoo that's safe for puppies, a brush and comb, a nail trimmer, and any specific supplies needed for your puppy's breed. (See chapter 10 for more on grooming.)

- **Identification.** Pick up a tag for his collar (available at most pet-supply stores) and make sure that both your cell phone and your home phone numbers are on it.

- **Pooper-scooper.** For backyard cleanups. You can also use plastic grocery bags to clean up after your dog.

- **Rectal thermometer.** A rectal thermometer (the kind used for human babies) is important in case your puppy doesn't feel well. Normal temperature is from 101 to 102 degrees Fahrenheit.

- **Toys.** Pick out several indestructible, safe toys.

It's much easier if you do this shopping before you pick up your puppy. That way, once you're home with him, you can stay home.

Puppyproofing Your Home

Puppies are curious creatures and can turn just about anything into a toy. Although chewing up a cardboard box won't hurt your puppy or cause any more damage than making a mess, many household items are harmful to him. Plus, replacing chewed-up shoes, television remote controls, and cell phones is expensive.

You can prevent a lot of damage and potential harm by puppyproofing your house prior to bringing home your puppy. Look at things from your puppy's perspective (and height) and put away anything dangling or tempting.

Make sure that all dangerous substances are out of reach or behind childproof locks.

- In the kitchen, those include candy (especially chocolate, which is toxic to dogs), oven cleaners, floor cleaning and waxing products, insect sprays and traps, and rodent traps.

- In the bathroom, dangerous products include toilet-bowl cleaners; shower, sink, and floor cleaners; makeup; hair-care products; medicines; vitamins; and bath products.

- In the living room and family areas, make sure that cigarettes and other smoking products are out of reach. Pens, felt-tipped markers, and craft supplies should be put away when not in use.

- Many houseplants can be dangerous, including ivy, dieffenbachia, and many flowering bulbs, including daffodils and tulips.

If your puppy gets into something he shouldn't, call your veterinarian right away. If the vet isn't immediately available, call the ASPCA's Poison Control Hotline at 888-426-4435. There is a fee, but they'll connect you to experts in poison control.

Golden Retriever–Labrador Retriever mix, 8 weeks old

Making Your Yard Safe

You need to make sure your yard is just as safe as your house, especially since your puppy may occasionally spend some time alone outside once he's older. Just as you did in the house, take a look at your yard from your puppy's perspective.

The fence around your yard needs to be very secure. Block any holes in the fence where a small puppy could squeeze through. Block any gaps or holes under the fence, as curious puppies can be quite determined to get out. Make sure that the fence is tall enough that a curious puppy can't jump or climb over it.

Put away all gardening equipment, including tools, gloves, and other chewable items. Fence off your flower and vegetable gardens so that the puppy doesn't inadvertently destroy all your hard work. Make sure that all yard chemicals such as fertilizer, herbicides, and other toxins are securely locked away. And then be cautious about using them around a puppy. Always read the labels thoroughly before using them.

Put away lawn chairs, hammocks, and other recreational items for the time being. Just bring them out when you're going to use them. You can teach your puppy to leave them alone later, but for now, preventing problems from occurring is best.

Encourage all family members to get into the habit of putting away all tools, toys, and other personal items when they are through using them in the backyard. Kids' toys are a puppy's favorite things to chew on because the toys smell strongly of the kids.

Make sure there are no poisonous plants in your yard that the puppy might nibble on. Check the ASPCA's Web site, www.aspca.org, for a list of poisonous plants.

English Shepherd, 8 weeks old

Bringing Home Your New Puppy

Bring home your new puppy when you will be able to spend a couple of days with him. A Friday is great if you normally work Monday through Friday. This way, the two of you can get to know each other and he can feel more secure before you have to resume your normal schedule.

Make sure that you have everything you need before you pick up your puppy. You're going to want to come straight home without stopping anywhere once you have the puppy, so double-check all your supplies first.

Have a crate in your car, with a soft blanket on the bottom. Toss a couple of towels in the car, too, in case the puppy gets carsick. Puppies tend to worry and stress out when they leave the only home they have known, and stress can lead to carsickness.

> **"Make sure that you have everything you need before you pick up your puppy."**

Ask the breeder not to feed the puppy if you're coming to get him in the morning. Then he is less apt to get carsick with an empty tummy. If you're coming to get him in the afternoon, ask her to feed the puppy a small breakfast, just enough to tide him over until he gets to your house—his new home. Once your puppy is home, take him directly to the place where you want him to relieve himself. Walk him around, but don't play with him. When he relieves himself, praise him. (Housetraining is explained in chapter 3.)

Once in the house, offer him a drink of water, and in an hour or so, let him have something to eat. Then, over the next couple of days, you can introduce him to what will become his normal routine. (See chapter 10 for specific information on feeding your puppy.)

West Highland White Terrier, 14 weeks old

Great Pyrenees

Chapter 2
Your New Family Member

Meeting Your Family

The new little life that you bring home is just a baby and full of potential. During the first few days at home, she will need to learn where she sleeps and where she hangs out during the day.

Your puppy also needs to meet everyone in the family and then learn what they smell and sound like and how each person acts towards her. However, if everyone in the family tries to hold her, pet her, and play with her all at the same time, she's going to feel overwhelmed.

Talk to everyone in the family before you bring home the puppy. Make sure everyone understands that only a couple people will go get the puppy while other family members remain at home. Then when the puppy arrives, people should not run out to greet her.

When your puppy arrives home, take her outside to relieve herself, give her a chance to relax and have something to eat, and then take her out to relieve herself again. Afterwards the family members can all sit on the floor. Let the puppy wander from person to person, greeting each one and getting petted by one person at a time.

All play with the puppy should be gentle. Don't allow anyone to play tug of war with the puppy because that teaches her to use her strength against people. Wrestling is another game that you shouldn't play as this teaches the puppy to fight you. Instead, play fetch and hide-and-seek games, and teach her the names of her toys. Teach her that people will be gentle with her and in return she should be gentle with people.

Border Collie, 5 weeks old

39

Labrador Retriever–Golden Retriever mix, 3 years old, and Labrador Retriever, 8 weeks old

Introducing Your Puppy to a Dog at Home

The preparations for your puppy should begin long before you bring your puppy home. If you have a dog at home, she is used to your attentions, and if she's an only dog, she's been the center of your attention. Bringing a puppy into the house is a drastic change for her.

If your older dog is well socialized to other dogs, she is more likely to be friendly to the puppy. Take the time to walk your older dog around places where she'll meet other dogs. Let her sniff other dogs who are friendly and well behaved, and ideally let them play, too.

Find a friend or acquaintance with a puppy and introduce your older dog to the puppy at a park or at your friend's home. Make a big deal over your older dog as she meets the puppy by saying, "Go say hi to the puppy, Sweetie. Good girl to be nice to the puppy!" Don't allow yourself to become distracted by the puppy's charms; this is all about making your older dog feel good about herself!

Then, when you bring the puppy home, have a family member meet you at the park with your older dog so you can introduce the two dogs in a place away from the house. Let them say hi, praise the older dog for being a good big sister, and let them sniff each other. When all seems calm, take them both home.

Over the next few days and weeks, make sure the older dog gets special attention. The puppy will be the focus of all the oohs and ahhhs, so make sure everyone spends time with the older dog, too. Take her for walks without the puppy, play ball with her, and give her some nice tummy rubs. After all, even though she's older, she's still very special.

Introducing Your Other Pets

If at all possible, give your puppy at least a day to get used to her new home before introducing your other pets. Meeting the family members and your other dog is quite enough for her for the first day. However, on her second or third day in your home you can introduce your cat, rabbit, ferret, or other pets.

Either hold your puppy in your arms or put a leash on her when you introduce her to the other pets in the family so you can prevent her from chasing them. Many breeds of dogs were originally bred for hunting and have a very strong prey drive (the desire to chase animals who run away). Unfortunately, the excitement of the chase can also cause these dogs to harm the animals if they catch them. Although your puppy is small, if she learns to chase your other pets now, then she will continue to do this when she grows up.

Instead, teach your puppy to behave gently with the cat, rabbit, and other pets. Let her smell the pets, telling her in a soft voice, "Be gentle. Good girl to be gentle," but use your hands or a leash to prevent her from chasing them. If the cat dashes away, as cats often do, then you will have a hard time restraining your puppy from following. Your puppy will really want to chase the running cat, but let her know it's not allowed by restraining her and if possible, distracting her.

“Teach your puppy to behave gently with the cat, rabbit, and other pets.”

If some of your smaller pets are caged, don't let your puppy harass them outside of the cage. If she barks, paws at the cage, chews on the bars, or otherwise makes their life miserable, then they will be stressed. After all, the cage is their home.

Border Collies, 15 months old and 6 weeks old

Australian Shepherd, 14 weeks old

Choosing Your Puppy's Name

A decade ago, the most popular dog names were King and Bear for male dogs and Brandy and Amber for female dogs. Today, Max, Jake, Buddy, and Sam are the most common names for male dogs, and the most common names for female dogs are Maggie, Molly, Lady, Sadie, and Lucy.

Other dog owners prefer more inventive or unique names. Some pick names derived from their professions, like Doc for the Beagle who belongs to a physician or PT for the physical therapist who shares his home with an Irish Setter. A science fiction fan named his mixed breed Hal, after the talking supercomputer in *2001: A Space Odyssey,* and a *Star Trek* enthusiast named her dog Bashir, after a charismatic character on *Star Trek: Deep Space Nine.* Names can come from anywhere if you have some imagination.

Make sure the name you choose fits your dog both today and ten to fourteen years from now. Calling a tiny puppy Itsy Bitsy Baby is fine now, but are you going to be happy calling that name a few years from now? Especially out in public?

You also want to choose a name that suits your dog. Many dog owners like to have several names in mind and then get to know the puppy over the first few days the puppy is home. Then, as they see the puppy's personality, they can choose the name that fits her best. For example, Riker is an Australian Shepherd who is an outgoing and affectionate charmer. He's named for the *Star Trek* character of the same name who shares those personality traits.

Don't give your puppy a negative name. Dogs named Killer, Trouble, and Fang tend to live up to those names if for no other reason than these names bring up negative thoughts. However, positive names such as Bubbles, Sweetie, and Beauty make you smile.

Rottweilers, 7 weeks old

Limiting Your Puppy's Freedom

Puppies have no idea that things in this world may be dangerous nor do they understand that you work hard so that you can have some nice possessions. Kate Abbott, of Kindred Spirits Dog Training in Vista, California, says this about her experience with training puppies, "Puppies live in the moment. Something may be fun to rip apart or pull the stuffing out of, and they will do that. But they aren't worried about any consequences."

It's important then that you become your puppy's protector. Protect her from herself, as well as the world around her, by limiting her access to things that could harm her or that she could destroy.

In chapter 3, you will learn what a crate is and how to use it to help limit your puppy's freedom. But baby gates can also help. Put baby gates across hallways to limit a puppy's freedom. Close bedroom doors, too, so she can't wander into them and discover shoes, dirty socks, and the kids' toys.

Exercise pens, also called x-pens, are portable fences and work just like playpens do for human toddlers. The toddler (or puppy) has room to play yet is still restrained so she can't get into trouble. You can easily move the x-pen so the puppy can be in the same room with you.

Preventing your puppy from getting into trouble now will also have a positive effect on her future behavior. If your puppy never discovers how much fun it is to rip apart a sofa cushion, for example, she will never develop that bad habit.

Continue limiting your puppy's freedom until she is well trained and mentally mature. For most puppies, this means until she's 18 to 24 months old.

Your Puppy Needs Her Own Bed

Ideally, your puppy should sleep in your bedroom with you. By spending eight hours a night in the same room, your puppy can hear you, smell you, and take comfort from your closeness. Your puppy should not sleep *in* your bed, however. She needs her own bed, which should be her crate.

If she sleeps in your bed, you could inadvertently harm the puppy. You could roll over in your sleep and pin your puppy or crush her. The puppy could also disrupt your sleep by moving around, trying to play with you, or even licking your nose. The puppy will not stay in your bed, either, and could end up in trouble: chewing your shoes, chewing on the carpet, or even having a housetraining accident.

> **"Sleeping in the crate will also help your puppy develop bowel and bladder control."**

However, when your puppy is in her crate in the bedroom with you, you can still be close to her but she will disrupt your sleep much less. Now granted, for the first few weeks she will need to go outside at least once per night. However, when she wants to play, you can simply tell her in a no-nonsense voice, "That's enough."

Sleeping in the crate will also help your puppy develop bowel and bladder control. Puppies are born with the instinct to keep their bed clean, so if the crate is your puppy's bed, she will try hard not to soil it. It's your responsibility to make sure she gets outside to relieve herself on a regular basis.

Restraining your puppy's freedom by crating her at bedtime will also help prevent problem chewing at night when you can't supervise her. This behavior usually peaks between the ages of 4 and 5 months when the puppy is teething, and then again at about 9 to 10 months when the puppy is exploring her world.

Rottweiler, 7 weeks old

Maltese, 12 weeks old

Why Is Your Puppy Crying?

Your first few days, and even weeks, together can be difficult for both your puppy and you. Your puppy has left her Mom and littermates, and she has no idea where she is or what is happening to her. She may be worried, insecure, and at times even frightened. You have a new puppy and want to do the best for her, but you may feel overwhelmed. Don't worry; within a week or two you will be able to decipher her verbalizations and will understand what she's trying to say.

Your puppy may cry when she's hungry. With her Mom, she knew how to get food; she would nurse. Now she's not sure how to make food appear and although she will eventually learn when mealtimes are, right now she has no idea. So offer meals on schedule, but then give her something safe to chew on in between meals.

She may also whine when she's lonely. Provide toys for her to play with and spend plenty of time with her, but again, do not come running every time she cries. She needs to learn how to cope with being alone now and then.

She will also make noise when she needs to go outside to relieve herself and you will quickly learn which sounds she makes for that. Make sure you respond to those sounds and reinforce this behavior by praising her for telling you she needs to go outside.

Your puppy will also cry when she hurts herself and you will know when this happens because her cries will mirror her hurt. Respond to these cries right away so you can see what she has done to herself and can immediately provide the care she needs.

Puppies Just Want to Have Fun

Many puppy owners seem to feel that their puppies are out to get them because they think the puppies purposely chew up the remote control or the cell phone. Although at times it may seem this way, puppies really aren't thinking that much about what they chew. Instead, puppies are attracted to things that smell good, and the remote and cell phones both smell like you. After all, you handle these items fairly often.

That's why puppies also chew on shoes and socks and the kids' toys. Puppies raid trash cans for the same reason.

Puppies will repeatedly go after things that are fun to destroy. When your puppy pulls the stuffing out of the sofa cushions, she is having fun. She can shake the cushion, pull the stuffing out, and then do it again. This action is self-rewarding; she has fun.

That's why puppies raid the trash can, too. When she can rip up some paper or when she finds treasures (to her!) in the kitchen trash can, she is rewarded for those behaviors by having fun.

You definitely need to prevent these behaviors, though, before they become bad habits. Once your puppy learns that raiding trash cans and tearing up sofa cushions is fun, you'll have a difficult time stopping this behavior in the future.

Stop the behaviors by preventing them—puppyproofing your house and yard, limiting her freedom—and then by supervising her when she's allowed to follow you around the house and yard. When she sticks her nose where it doesn't belong or picks up something she shouldn't, use a firm voice and tell her, "That's not yours! No!" and then walk her away. Show her what she should pick up—her toy or a chewie—and then praise her for having that by saying, "Good girl to get a toy!"

Miniature Dachshund–English Cocker Spaniel mix, 7 weeks old

Spaniel mix, 14 weeks old

Teaching Your Puppy and Children to Play Nicely

Initially, kids and puppies seem like ideal playmates; after all, they are both young and full of energy. Unfortunately, as with so many things, real life isn't as idyllic.

Puppies look upon children as littermates to wrestle with or as something to chase and catch. Puppies have no idea that their sharp, little puppy teeth can cause harm to people and, unfortunately, when the kids scream and run, the puppies will chase even more.

Children need to learn to be calm and gentle with a puppy. No running, no screaming and hollering, no wrestling, and no teasing. Kids should never lie down on the floor and allow a puppy to climb all over them; instead, they can sit on the floor and the puppy can climb into their laps. The best games for kids and puppies are fetch and hide-and-seek (see chapter 6).

Use the leash to restrain your puppy so you can prevent her from chasing the children, both in the house and out in the yard. If your puppy jumps up on the kids, tell the puppy, "No jump!" and shape her into a sit (see chapters 4 and 8).

Never leave children and your puppy alone together without adult supervision. Unfortunately, children will be children and may misbehave—they all do sometimes—and the puppy will be a puppy and act as puppies do. Children and puppies can be good friends. But it doesn't happen automatically; they need adult supervision and help, and both the kids and the puppy need to learn how to behave themselves around each other.

Being a Good Puppy Parent

It's important to establish yourself as your puppy's parent very early in your relationship. Even if you want this puppy to grow up to be your best friend, you must be her parent first. She needs your guidance and maturity and later she can be your friend.

First of all, don't allow her to treat you as she did her littermates. She's not allowed to bite you, jump on you, chew on your hands or pant legs, or otherwise treat you as an equal. She can play with you, but she's never allowed to show you disrespect.

Have her sit (see chapters 4 and 8) while you fix her food. Then when you're ready to feed her, give her permission to go eat. Do not allow her to jump all over you for her food or try and knock the bowl out of your hands.

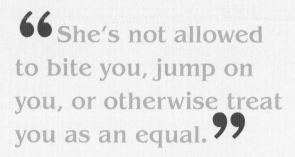

"She's not allowed to bite you, jump on you, or otherwise treat you as an equal."

Teach her to sit at all doorways (see chapter 9) and to wait for permission to go through open doors. This allows you to control access to the house; after all, you may want to towel her off before she comes in from outside. Teaching her to sit at doorways and wait for permission to go through the door can also help prevent her from dashing out the front door or gate and running into the street.

You control the toys. You need the ability to give your puppy toys and then take them away. Do not allow her to growl at you or guard the toys. One day she may chew on something that is potentially dangerous and you'll need to take it away. If she growls or snaps at you, call a professional dog trainer for help right away.

Begin teaching household rules (see chapter 4) and enforce them. You follow rules of polite social behavior, and so should your puppy. Be her parent.

Pit Bull Terrier, 22 weeks old

Introducing the Buckle Collar and Leash

A buckle collar is a nylon, leather, or cotton-web collar that fits around your puppy's neck and then fastens with either a metal or plastic buckle. Although most of these collars are adjustable, you may need to get her two or three different collars as she grows up.

You can use a nylon, leather, or cotton-web leash, too. A four- or six-foot length is good because this gives you some length of leash to work with as you begin teaching your puppy.

To introduce the buckle collar to your puppy, put it on her just before she does something that she is going to enjoy, such as playtime or dinner. This fun activity will distract her, so she is less likely to try and scratch the collar off. If she does try to scratch at it, toss a toy to her to distract her from the collar.

As soon as your puppy is comfortable with the collar, snap the leash on to it and let it drag behind her. Let her just get used to the feel of it as it follows her. She may step on it and that's OK. If she tries to chew on it, dip it in some white vinegar so it tastes bad. Always take the leash off when you can't supervise your puppy.

When the leash no longer bothers her, hold on to it and begin letting her feel that you have hold of it. Hold a good treat in your hand and then use it as a lure in front of her nose and back away from her, encouraging her to follow you. If she dashes away, you have the leash to stop her. But if she follows you, praise her and give her the treat.

Maltipoo, 14 weeks old

Labrador Retriever, 12 weeks old

Putting Identification on Your Puppy

As soon as your puppy is used to her buckle collar, put an identification tag on it. This should have your home and cell phone numbers on it. If you haven't chosen a name for your puppy yet, that's fine. The phone numbers will get your puppy home if she gets lost.

When your puppy goes to the veterinarian's office for her first checkup and vaccinations (see chapter 10), ask your vet about microchipping. A microchip is a tiny computer chip (about the size of a grain of rice) that is injected under a dog's skin between her shoulder blades. The microchip is coded, and your vet will give you the information to register this code, including where to send the information and any requirements the database may have. When a microchip reader is waved over the puppy's shoulders, that code is read and you will be notified that your puppy has been found.

Several types of microchips are available, but many veterinarians use the type made by HomeAgain. The chip is easily read by most scanners used by veterinarians, animal-control shelters, and humane societies. This chip has been used for many years and longterm studies show that it is safe to use in dogs of all sizes. For more information, go to www.homeagain.com.

You should also take photos of your puppy and continue to take pictures as she grows up. If your puppy is ever lost, you can use these photos on flyers to post in the neighborhood. But you can also use them to identify your dog in case someone picks her up and you need to prove that you are her owner.

Obviously, preventing your puppy from ever straying is the most important thing you can do. But taking precautions—such as keeping an ID tag on your puppy and having her microchipped—are also vital to keeping her safe.

Labrador Retriever, 12 weeks old

Don't Worry; Relax and Laugh!

New puppy owners often worry so much about not making any mistakes with their puppy that they forget to have fun with her. Puppies are young for a very short time; they grow up so fast that you should take the time to enjoy puppyhood.

Rediscover the world around you as your puppy learns what it is. Enjoy the colors of a butterfly as your puppy tries to chase it. Pick a flower and let your puppy sniff it. Watch the sea gulls fly as your puppy tries to figure out what they are.

Your puppy is also a lot of fun. Sit on the floor and show your puppy an empty cardboard box. Let her climb into it, grab and shake it, and even chew on it. When we were kids, cardboard boxes were toys for us, too. We turned them into playhouses or spaceships or caves. But once we grew up, we lost that imagination and sense of fun. A puppy can bring it back.

Puppies also offer unconditional love. Puppies don't care what you look like or how much money you make; they have no agenda and no guile. They just want your affection and love and are more than willing to give it right back to you. There is nothing quite like having a warm, affectionate puppy fall asleep on your lap.

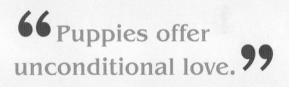
"Puppies offer unconditional love."

Puppies are also good for you. When you take a puppy for a walk, you get exercise. You talk with the people who stop to pet your puppy and these social interactions are excellent for your mental health. In addition, the love and affection from your puppy is good for both your mental and physical health.

So take the time to enjoy your puppy by playing with her and loving her.

Havanese, 15 weeks old

Chapter 3

Housetraining Your Puppy

Housetraining Goals

As you begin housetraining your puppy, which should begin the day you bring your puppy home, keep some basic goals in mind. First, you want your puppy to relieve himself outside rather than inside the house. Although this may seem obvious, too many dog owners put up with "accidents" without doing anything constructive to change their dog's behavior.

Another goal is to teach your dog to relieve himself on command. If you're in a hurry or are going to take the dog inside a building, you can ask him to relieve himself and he will.

Most dog owners like to teach their dog to relieve himself in a particular spot in the backyard rather than all over the backyard. This is a worthwhile goal especially if you have children in the family and would like to keep some parts of the yard clean.

It's also important that your puppy is comfortable relieving himself on command in places other than the backyard. He should be able to relieve himself on command while out on a walk, before he goes in to puppy class, and whenever you ask. If he's taught to go only in the backyard, then you will have problems later because he will think that's the only place he's allowed to go. Teach him this skill just as you do the housetraining at home, by following the instructions you learn here.

Teaching your dog to feel comfortable in a crate is also a useful goal. The crate serves as a bed and a place of refuge, and also teaches bowel and bladder control, which is useful should you travel with your dog. Crate training also prevents problem behaviors from beginning.

You may have some other housetraining goals, so think about this aspect of your dog's training. What would you like your puppy to know and do as he grows up?

Labrador Retriever–Golden Retriever cross, 8 weeks old

Cardigan Welsh Corgi, 9 weeks old

Incorporating Longterm Goals into Your Housetraining

Dogs are creatures of habit, so you should teach your puppy housetraining skills in order to make sure he continues to use these skills when he's a full-grown dog. Changing the rules later is very difficult.

Shelly Cameron, a retired dog trainer from Orlando, Florida, says, "Not too long ago a former client called me. I had helped her teach her English Springer Spaniel, Amber, to use a cat litter box in the house. My client lived in an apartment and I warned her she may not be happy about this arrangement in the future, but she was emphatic this was what she wanted. Well, now Amber is 3 years old, full grown, and is producing a great deal of urine and feces each day—as a dog of this size will—and my former client wants to change the housetraining rules and have the dog relieve herself outside only. Although the dog is relieving herself outside, she also expects to be able to use her litter box and when the box is not available, is relieving herself on the floor where the box used to be."

Cameron continues, "My former client is upset because the dog urine and feces are smelling up her apartment and ruining the floors. However, I told her this isn't the dog's fault; the dog was doing what she had been taught to do."

None of us is very good at predicting the future; we don't know how our lives will change in the coming years. But try to think about life with your dog and the potential future the two of you may have. What housetraining skills will be important? Make sure you incorporate all these skills as you begin teaching your puppy.

Using a Crate for Your Puppy's Bed

Dogs like to sleep in small, cavelike places (dens). Dens provide security from outside threats and provide the puppy with a place where he can relax and sleep without worrying about being disturbed. Dogs are born with these instincts; that's why so many dogs curl up under the foot of the recliner or sleep under the coffee table.

Commercial crates were originally designed for shipping animals. If you watch any of the zoo shows on television, you can see everything from birds to cats and even meerkats being transported in plastic boxes. About twenty-five years ago, these crates were gaining in popularity as tools for preventing bad behaviors in dogs. Previously most puppies learned their housetraining skills in a haphazard manner, often by being exiled to the backyard. But housetraining became much easier with the crate because it uses a puppy's instinct to keep his bed clean.

> **" The crate uses a puppy's instinct to keep his bed clean. "**

A number of different brands and types of crates are available. The original plastic crate has a top piece and bottom piece that are held together with bolts that you can tighten and loosen by hand, and it has a grill door. Wire crates are made from heavy-gauge wire and are more cagelike than the plastic crates. These are great for dogs who need more ventilation (dogs with short muzzles, such as Pugs and Pekingese) or dogs living in hot, humid climates.

Choose a crate that will give your puppy room to lie down, stretch out, and get comfortable. However, if you get one that is big enough for him when he's full grown, divide the crate into smaller sections right now so your puppy won't relieve himself in a back corner and then still have room to get away from his mess.

Cavalier King Charles Spaniel, 5 weeks old

Australian Shepherd, 8 weeks old

Introducing the Crate to Your Puppy

To introduce your puppy to the crate, which should occur during your puppy's first day at home, open the crate door and block it open so it cannot swing shut. Toss one of your puppy's favorite toys (squeaky toy, rope, or his ball) towards the crate. When he gets his toy, cheer him on by saying, "Yeah! Good boy to get your toy!" Repeat the game by tossing the toy around the outside and inside of the crate.

For your next crate-training session, take a handful of small treats and toss them into the crate. When he goes in to eat them, close the door behind him. Give him a chance to discover that the door is closed, praise him, wait five seconds, and then open the door. Repeat this a few more times, gradually increasing the time while making sure you open the door only when the puppy is quiet. Never open the door when he's throwing a temper tantrum or barking.

Then begin feeding your puppy in his crate. Place the food bowl in the back of the crate and let the puppy go in after it as you tell him, "Sweetie, go to bed." The food serves as the reward. Initially, don't close the door after him; let him go in and out as he pleases. But after a couple of meals, close the door after him. When he finishes eating and turns around and discovers the door is closed, wait a few seconds before you open the door.

Most puppies accept the crate quickly after these few training sessions. A few puppies are resistant, but even they will accept it with some meals, toys, treats, and praise. After all, when puppies are in a crate, they are not far removed from being in a den (or whelping box) with their mother.

Using the Crate Wisely

Your puppy should spend the night in the crate. This isn't the time to let your puppy climb into bed with you or sleep on the floor in the bedroom; instead, the puppy should sleep in the crate so he can develop the bowel and bladder control needed to make it through the night. It can take several months for your puppy to develop this kind of control, though, so be patient.

Most 8- to 10-week-old puppies can sleep through the night with only one trip outside, and many can make it all night (six hours more or less) by 12 weeks of age. But every puppy is different. During the day, puppies will have to go outside more often and will always have to go out after eating, drinking, playing, and after waking up from a nap.

If your puppy is fussy and restless in the crate, take him directly outside to relieve himself. If you let him out because you think he needs to relieve himself and he doesn't go, then bring him inside and put him back in the crate. If you let him run around the house, he may have an accident on the carpet or floor.

If you need to keep your puppy in the crate for a few hours during the day, give him one of the toys that dispenses food or treats. Put some treats or dry kibble inside the toy and give it to your dog when you put him in the crate.

During the day, you can crate young puppies for an hour at a time here and there throughout the day, but as a general rule puppies should not spend more than four hours total in the crate.

Labrador Retriever, 10 weeks old

Chihuahua

Don't Abuse the Crate

Using the crate to housetrain your puppy doesn't mean that your puppy should spend his life in the crate. Never use the crate to "store" the puppy; instead, use it as a training tool. The puppy still needs to spend most of his time outside of the crate with you, learning the rules of his world and being loved by you.

In addition, do not use the crate to punish your puppy. If you walk into the living room and see a puddle on the floor, don't drag the puppy to his crate and toss him in as you scold him. (See chapter 4 for advice on how to train your puppy when he makes a mistake.)

Crate training focuses on using the puppy's natural instincts to want a clean den; if you use the crate as punishment, the puppy will resist going into it and once in will whine, cry, or bark to get back out. Once the puppy is afraid of the crate or dislikes it, you'll have a hard time changing his mind.

Although you should never use the crate as punishment, using it as a place for a timeout is acceptable. The difference between a timeout and a punishment is your attitude and bearing. For example, don't toss the puppy in the crate and slam the door, nor stand outside the crate yelling. Those actions are negative and will cause the puppy to dislike the crate.

However, if your puppy gets overexcited during playtime in the house and can't calm down, you can take him by the collar and calmly put him in his crate and leave him there for fifteen minutes. This timeout in the crate gives him a chance to calm down. There is no yelling, no fighting, no slamming of the crate door; all is calm.

Establishing a Schedule

Puppies must relieve themselves at certain times, including after waking from a nap, after eating, after playing, and every few hours throughout the day. By knowing this, you can establish a schedule to make sure your puppy gets outside regularly so that you can prevent housetraining accidents, so you can teach your puppy where he should relieve himself, and so you can praise him for going where and when you want him to go.

To establish a schedule, list the things you do with your puppy and when you normally do them. When do you brush your puppy? When do you play with him the most? When does he have his meals? At what time do you walk him? Jot these things and times down on a piece of paper.

Now you also know that your puppy needs to relieve himself after each meal, after waking up from a nap, immediately after getting up in the morning, and last thing before you go to bed at night. He will also need to go outside after an energetic play session. When do those things normally happen? Jot down each item and the times.

Now put all these items in order, time-wise, from the first thing your puppy needs to do in the morning after you wake up (go outside) to the last thing at night before you go to bed (go outside!).

> **Make sure your puppy gets outside regularly so that you can prevent housetraining accidents.**

Now list all of your commitments. When do the kids get up? When do they need to leave for school? Jot down all of your family's regular commitments and activities. List all of these things and put them in time order. Now combine your lists—your family's and the puppy's. This is your daily schedule—stick to it as much as you can.

Cardigan Welsh Corgi, 9 weeks old

Miniature Dachshund–English Cocker Spaniel mix, 7 weeks old

Teaching Your Puppy to "Go" on Command

Puppies (and dogs) don't always need to relieve themselves according to a schedule, so teaching your puppy a word or phrase that means, "Try to relieve yourself right now," is important. When your puppy tries to relieve himself at your request, you can feel assured that your puppy doesn't have to go when you put him in his crate, let him play in the house, or go into someone else's home.

The word or phrase should be something everyone in the family is willing to say. For example, if you choose "Go tinkle," your husband or teenagers may refuse to use the word "tinkle" and may make up their own phrases, which will only confuse the puppy. You will also use this phrase for the rest of your dog's life, so choose your wording wisely.

Many people use the phrase "Go potty"; however, a phrase such as "Get busy" is much less noticeable. You will use this phrase when you take your puppy outside to relieve himself. Wait while he sniffs and finds the right spot. While he's going, tell him quietly, "Get busy!" Your voice needs to be heard but not so loud that you interrupt what he's doing. When he finishes, praise him enthusiastically with your first words being, "Good boy to get busy!"

After a week or so of praising him for relieving himself, then start telling him to go— using your potty phrase—as you take him outside. Continue to praise him as he relieves himself.

Keep in mind that you are not ordering your puppy to go potty; you shouldn't sound like a military drill instructor. Nor are you pleading with your puppy to go. Instead, use a normal tone of voice. When praising him for relieving himself, use a happy tone of voice.

Going Outside with Your Puppy

Where do you want your puppy to relieve himself? Choose wisely now because once you teach him to go in this spot, changing it later is very difficult. He should have easy access to the spot and it shouldn't be too far away from the door where he goes outside.

When the schedule shows that your puppy should go outside, or when you see your puppy sniffing the floor, or when he asks to go outside, then go out with him. Do not send the puppy outside by himself! When he's outside and you're inside, you cannot teach him. Plus, if you praise him when he comes to the door to come back in, you are rewarding him for coming to the door rather than for relieving himself. That's not the message you are hoping to convey.

In addition, if you send your puppy outside by himself, you have no idea if he's relieved himself or not. He could come inside with a full bladder and then relieve himself on the carpet. Go outside to teach him and to make sure he completely relieves himself.

Once you take your puppy to his spot, just hold his leash and wait. Hopefully, he will have a full bladder and will go. When he's going, praise him softly using his command, "Get busy! Good boy to get busy!" But don't praise him so loudly that you distract and interrupt him; this is the time to reinforce the idea that the command "Get busy" means to relieve himself.

Once your puppy understands this lesson, then begin asking him to go potty on command in other places—such as when out on a walk or outside the veterinarian's office—so that he understands the training applies in other places.

French Bulldogs

Chesapeake Bay Retriever

Praising the Behaviors You Want to Happen Again

People who study behavior—whether it's the behavior of dogs, horses, or people—know that those behaviors that are rewarded will happen again. The behaviors may be self-rewarded—the taste and pleasure of a hot fudge sundae is rewarding to many people—or someone else may give the reward, such as praise and a bonus check from your boss.

The same is true for your dog, except the rewards for his housetraining efforts will include your voice telling him "Good boy to get busy!" as well as petting, a toss of his favorite ball, or a special treat. Notice these are all things dogs usually like; a reward doesn't work if the puppy doesn't like it. This means you need to know your puppy. Is he food-motivated? Is a tennis ball a better reward than a squeaky toy? Find a few things your puppy really likes and then make sure you have at least one of those things on hand at all times.

> " A reward doesn't work if the puppy doesn't like it. "

You will use these rewards whenever your puppy does something you want him to do. When he goes outside with you and relieves himself in the correct spot, praise him by saying, "Good boy to get busy! Yeah, good job!" while you also pet him and give him a treat. After a few repetitions, he will understand that relieving himself in that spot causes good things to come his way.

Don't hesitate to exuberantly praise him with, "Yeah! What a wonderful puppy to get busy!" This is not the time to skimp on praise. After all, let him know you're really happy that he's relieved himself here and not on the carpet!

When he's all done relieving himself and you've praised him, then he can run around, play with you, or catch the ball for a few minutes. This playtime is also a reward.

Preventing Housetraining Accidents

Preventing accidents from happening is a huge part of housetraining. Puppies tend to return to the same "bathroom" spot (or spots) time after time. Yelling at your puppy when you find a puddle or pile in the house will not work (will not teach him what to do instead), so you need to prevent accidents from occurring while you teach him where he's supposed to go to relieve himself.

Remember to focus this training on teaching your puppy what to do, where to do it, and when to do it. You should not direct your training at what not to do because, after all, puppies do have to relieve themselves.

After your puppy goes outside and relieves himself, he can be in the room with you but do not let him roam the house unsupervised. If you are in a relatively small room where you can see your puppy at all times, he can have free run of that room. If you're in a large room or a room with large pieces of furniture where the puppy can sneak away, then have him on a leash and keep him close to you.

Close the door to the room so your puppy can't wander away, or put up a baby gate across the doorways or hallways. You want to make sure your puppy can't disappear from view. If you're busy and cannot supervise the puppy, put him in his crate or in a safe place outside in the yard.

Untrained puppies who have free run of the house can get into way too much trouble, and unless you catch them in the act, you can't do anything about it later. They can have housetraining accidents, chew on electrical cords, destroy the television remote, raid the trash cans, and so much more.

Bulldog

Chinese Crested Powderpuff

Chapter 4

Teaching Household Rules

Household Rules Are Vital

Do you like dogs on your furniture? Do you mind having your puppy underfoot while you're cooking in the kitchen? Does the idea of your puppy dashing out the front door fill you with dread?

You can comfortably share your home with a canine companion as long as the dog understands some basic rules. If you don't have rules or if your dog ignores any rules you try to establish, well, then chaos is king (or queen!) and life with your dog is no fun.

You should begin teaching your puppy the rules of your household right away, as soon as she joins your family. Just as housetraining should begin immediately, so should this training. When the rules are taught from day one, then your puppy can't develop any undesirable habits that you will have to change later.

The household rules you establish (see "A Suggested List of Household Rules," later in this chapter) are totally up to you. The rules your neighbor has for her dog and her household may not fit your home and lifestyle at all, so don't worry about that. Instead, you should teach your puppy those things that are important to you.

Make sure that everyone in the household agrees to consistently enforce these rules. If you want to keep the dog off the living room sofa, but your son invites the dog up when he comes home from school, well, your dog is going to be very confused and she will behave erratically. She will continually try to get up on the sofa.

So talk to family members. What rules would they like the puppy to know, understand, and follow? What is important to you? Does everyone understand the importance of providing the puppy with consistency?

Siberian Husky, 13 weeks old

Avoiding Self-Rewarding Behaviors

Self-rewarding behaviors were discussed in chapter 2, but they bear mentioning again, especially as I discuss how to teach your puppy to observe household rules. Behavior experts know that behaviors that cause good or pleasurable things to happen right away are repeated. If you like chocolate cake, then when you eat a piece, the taste, texture, and feel of the cake will stimulate the pleasure centers of your brain. This causes you to want to eat this type of cake again; eating the cake becomes self-rewarding. Because weight gain happens later, it doesn't affect the pleasure of eating the cake.

Puppies can create many self-rewarding behaviors. Raiding the kitchen trash can and finding leftover bits of food is self-rewarding. Tearing up a roll of toilet paper and having a great old time doing it is self-rewarding. Dashing out the front door and then playing keep-away while your owner chases you is self-rewarding. Anything that gives a puppy pleasure is self-rewarding.

You cannot punish a puppy for these behaviors, because the pleasure of the rewards outweighs anything you do. Punishment will not change these behaviors at all, and your anger will simply threaten your relationship with your dog.

Instead, you must train your puppy to do other things (called *alternative behaviors*) and you need to prevent the self-rewarding behaviors from occurring. Put the trash cans out of reach, close the bathroom door, and teach your puppy to sit and stay at open doorways (keeping her on a leash, of course). By supervising your puppy, preventing things from happening, and then teaching your puppy alternative behaviors that result in praise from you, you can eliminate self-rewarding bad behaviors.

Cairn Terrier

Havanese, 1½ years old (left) and 5½ months old (right)

Your Home before and after Puppy

Adding a puppy to your home, family, and routine can be very disruptive, especially if you haven't had a dog in the family. As you think about establishing some household rules, think about your home and your routine before you brought home the puppy and the way things are now.

What changes has your puppy caused that you would like to decrease or eliminate? Obviously, your puppy (and even the dog she will grow up to become) will drag in dirt from outside, but you can always teach her to sit at the door and wait until someone towels off her paws. With training and consistency, you can easily make these things into household rules.

Some changes, especially those involving your time and commitment to the puppy, will not change. These responsibilities are a vital part of dog ownership, and hopefully over time you will look upon the time spent with your dog as a joy rather than a chore.

As you look at your home and routine, and think about what household rules will work best for your situation, don't forget to think about your dog as an adult. She may be a fifteen-pound puppy now, but how big is she going to be when grown up? And what is her adult coat going to be like? There's a big difference between having a fifteen-pound, fuzzy puppy on the sofa and having a hundred-pound, longhaired, shedding dog on the sofa.

Once you create a list of household rules and begin teaching them, don't change them later. As you saw with housetraining, changing a dog's behavior later is very difficult and is confusing to the dog. So think carefully before making a list of household rules.

A Suggested List of Household Rules

Every family and home is different, but here are some potential household rules for your puppy.

- **No jumping.** Don't allow your puppy to jump up on family members or on guests.

- **No begging.** Begging for food is annoying. In addition, it tends to lead to food stealing.

- **Leave trash cans alone.** That means the kitchen trash can as well as the ones in the bathrooms.

- **No chasing the cats.** Your cats can do anything they wish, but don't allow your dog to chase them.

- **Sit and wait at all doors and gates.** This means your puppy must sit and wait for permission to go through all doors and gates.

- **Stay out of the kitchen.** Not only is an underfoot puppy a potential safety hazard, but too many dogs also learn how to open cupboard doors.

This list doesn't include housetraining, of course, as that goes without saying. Now your list will be different because your routine, home, and likes and dislikes are different. But you can use this list as a starting point for creating your own list.

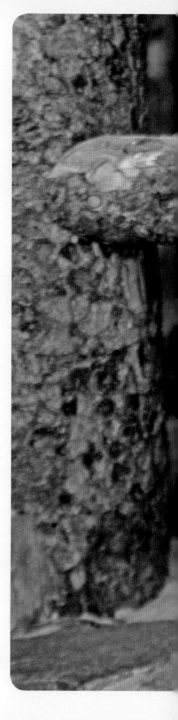

Bearded Collie

Shiba Inu, 20 weeks old

Teaching Your Puppy to Follow the Rules

As mentioned in chapter 1, your puppy's mom began teaching him when he was quite young. Through her efforts, he learned that he needed to follow some rules, including that he wasn't allowed to use his sharp little puppy teeth to hurt her.

As you begin to teach your puppy—both the household rules and the basic obedience skills—you're going to continue the training that his mother began. Momma dog used her voice to teach her puppy. When the puppy was good, she would murmur to him, and when he made a mistake, she would growl at him. He learned that a high-pitched voice was positive and a deep growl was a correction.

You can do the same thing. When your puppy walks past the trash can and picks up his toy, praise him in a happy tone of voice by saying, "Yeah! Good choice! Good boy!" If he sticks his nose in the trash can, stop this unwanted behavior with a deep, sharp tone of voice saying, "Ack! Get out of there!" Then walk your puppy to one of his toys and praise him when he picks it up by saying, "Here! Play with this instead. Good boy!"

Follow these simple procedures when teaching household rules to your puppy.

- Show him what to do and help him do it.

- Praise and reward him (with a toy or treat) for doing it.

- Prevent bad behaviors from happening.

- Interrupt bad behaviors when you catch your puppy in the act.

- Then show your puppy again what to do.

Never correct or punish your puppy for something that happened earlier. Your puppy thinks in the moment—the here and now—and corrections after the fact are not effective.

Sometimes Puppies Make Mistakes

Don't focus too much attention on any mistakes your puppy makes. With housetraining, if you scold your puppy for accidents, she will get sneaky and make mistakes behind the sofa. With household rules, if you get too upset, your puppy will begin to believe her name is "No, no, bad dog!"

Unfortunately, puppies do make mistakes. They don't know why we have all these rules. And if you scold your puppy too many times, or worse yet, if you get physical with her, she may think this is just the way things are. She may think that negative attention is better than being ignored, so she might continue the bad behavior just so she does get attention—any attention.

> **If you scold your puppy for accidents, she will get sneaky and make mistakes behind the sofa.**

If you find yourself yelling at your puppy all the time, losing your patience, or grabbing her because you're mad, then you need to change your approach to training. Use these methods to train your puppy and to help you respond more productively to her mistakes.

- Focus on giving your puppy praise, treats, and playtimes for good behavior.

- Help your puppy do what it is you want her to do.

- Prevent problem behaviors from happening.

- Ignore any bad behaviors that do happen.

- When your puppy makes a mistake, look upon it as a challenge to figure out how to prevent it from happening again.

When you decrease all the negative attention and reward good behavior, your puppy's behavior will change for the better.

Jack Russell Terrier

Pit Bull Terrier, 22 weeks old

Don't Ignore Good Behavior

You've likely heard the adage "The squeaky wheel gets the grease." This means that those people who speak up about problems get results. If you receive bad service at a business, you complain and hopefully something is done about it.

Unfortunately, most people are quick to complain but are not nearly as ready to praise good service. Even though praising the good things that happen is actually a better way to improve service, behaviorally, we tend not to do this.

Your puppy, however, cannot tolerate this type of a training technique. You can interrupt bad behavior that you catch happening, but you must praise and reward good behavior. Your puppy needs to know what you want her to do and she needs you to reinforce (praise) this behavior over and over again throughout puppyhood.

This repetition is important because puppies have short attention spans and the repeated reinforcements bring her back to what she should be doing. It's also necessary for your puppy's training because dogs learn through repetition.

Teach yourself to look for those things that your puppy is doing that you want her to continue doing. When she's chewing on her toy in the living room, praise her by saying, "Good girl! That's a good toy!" When she picks up her toy and not your shoes, tell her, "Good choice! Yeah!" When she asks to go outside to relieve herself, cheer her efforts with, "Yeah! Good girl to ask to go outside!"

Do not be the squeaky wheel towards your puppy; instead, be her cheerleader!

Don't Inadvertently Reward Bad Behavior

When your puppy's mom corrected him for using his sharp baby teeth too roughly, she used a deep, growly tone of voice to let her puppy know he made a mistake. Momma dog probably also showed her teeth in an ugly snarl. Your puppy knew exactly what it was that his mom was communicating to him.

Many puppy owners dislike using a rough tone of voice when talking to their puppies; some seem to think that a rough voice is mean or not nice. They prefer to use baby talk with the puppy or to console the puppy by using a soft voice when saying, "Oh, it's okay, Sweetie. I know you didn't mean to chew up my shoes."

That soft voice is not going to stop any bad behaviors. Instead, a soft voice is understood by your puppy as a neutral voice; it's not a correction and it's not praise. The attention your puppy receives from you while saying these soft words, however, is taken as positive reinforcement; after all, you picked the puppy up and cuddled her as you spoke to her. By using these words and actions, you are making sure these bad behaviors will continue and in all reality, they will get worse.

You must communicate very clearly with your puppy. In addition, it's up to you to make sure your puppy understands; your puppy cannot change who she is, therefore *you* must bridge the species communication gap.

Use a neutral, normal tone to ask your puppy to do something; use a higher pitched, happy tone of voice to praise her; and a deeper, growly tone of voice to let her know she made a mistake. Don't yell; volume is not necessary. The tone of voice that you use is what's important.

Labrador Retriever–wolf cross, 15 weeks old

Rottweiler, 7 weeks old

Teaching the Sit for Petting

You will need to use a few basic obedience exercises as you begin to teach your puppy the household rules that you want her to understand. The first exercise is *sit,* which means your dog should place her hips on the ground, keep her front end up, and hold still. Since your puppy doesn't understand these words, you need to show her what you mean. Follow these steps to teach your puppy how to sit for petting.

1. Put your puppy on her leash and then hold the leash in your left hand.

2. Hold a treat in your right hand and let your puppy sniff it.

3. As your puppy sniffs the treat, tell her, "Sweetie, sit."

4. Move the treat over her head slightly and back towards her shoulders. Her nose should follow the treat up.

5. Her hips will go down as her head comes up. As her hips hit the ground, praise her by saying, "Good sit!" and pop the treat in her mouth.

6. If she's wiggly, then use your leash hand to also hold her collar.

7. After she finishes the treat, tell her, "Sweetie, okay!" and let her get up.

Praise her again when she gets up. Repeat this exercise three of four times and then take a break.

When your puppy can hold the sit for a few seconds until you release her, begin to pet her while she's in the sit before you release her. Hold her collar with the hand holding the leash so you can make sure she remains in the sit, and then pet her with your other hand. Scratch her ears, stroke her neck and side, and pat her on the ribcage. She should now greet everyone while in a sit; no jumping on people allowed!

Teaching the Collar Touch

The second obedience exercise to teach your puppy is the *collar touch,* which teaches her to come to you for a treat and to sit while you touch her. She also needs to hold the sit until you release her. Far too many puppies think they can dash in, grab the treat, and then dash away again. The come command turns into a "keep-away game" rather than encouraging the puppy to "come to the owner and remain with the owner."

Have some really good treats at hand. Leftover chicken from last night's dinner or cheese works great, but cut them up into tiny bits. Follow these steps to teach the collar touch to your puppy.

1. Put the leash on your puppy and let her sniff the treats. Don't give her one yet, just let her know what you have.

2. Using the previous technique, have your puppy sit and then give her a treat. Release her from the sit and praise her enthusiastically.

3. Now have her sit, verbally praise her, and then touch her collar before you give her a treat. Then release her and praise her. Repeat this step three times and then take a break.

4. On your next training session, repeat the first three steps. But when you touch her collar, jiggle it and move it around her neck, then give her a treat and release her. Repeat a few times and then give her a break.

> **"All of these touches teach your puppy to come close and remain close to you."**

Over the next few days of training, touch her collar, wiggle it, snap the leash on and off, or touch your puppy's body with one hand before she gets her treat. All of these touches are necessary and will come in handy throughout your puppy's life because they teach her to come close and remain close to you, and they also prevent her from dashing away when you need to touch her.

Great Dane, 12 weeks old

Pug, 5 months old

Chapter 5

The Human– Animal Bond

Why Do We Bond with Dogs?

Americans own innumerable pets: dogs, cats, birds, hamsters, gerbils, horses, aquarium fish, as well as lizards and snakes. The total numbers probably range in the trillions of animals. Numerous studies over the last three decades have shown that in order to achieve good health, both mentally and physically, we need contact with other living things.

Researchers have recently discovered and named a childhood disorder called Nature Deficit Disorder. Children who lack a connection to other living things—plants and animals—can suffer from a number of problems, one of which is a disregard for the natural world and a lack of empathy for other living things. Children who have pets, however, rarely suffer from this disorder.

Of all our pets, dogs are able to wiggle their way into our hearts and homes more than any other pet. Through their ease in adapting to our lifestyles, their ability to communicate with us, and their desire to work for us, dogs have become our number-one companion animal.

Another factor that makes them attractive to us is their ability to form social ties and friendships. This ability enables domesticated dogs to feel comfortable in our families. Anyone who has watched a dog tolerate the attentions of a clumsy human toddler can immediately see that the dog knows that a toddler is a baby, like a puppy, and that babies don't yet understand the correct rules of social behavior.

All in all, we bond with dogs because they are a good fit with us. But most importantly, dogs love us, and we all need to feel loved.

Australian Cattle Dog, 18 weeks old

Maltipoo, 18 weeks old

How Is Bonding with Dogs Good for You?

We bond with our pets, especially our dogs, but how is this bond good for us? Some of the positive effects that pets provide for their owners include the following:

- Pets provide friendship and companionship.

- Pets alleviate loneliness.

- People need to feel needed, and our pets need us.

- Pets, especially dogs, cause us to be more active.

- We play and laugh with our pets, both of which are good for us.

- We need to touch other living things, and pets provide us with that benefit when we cuddle them.

- Dogs in particular make us feel more secure.

- Pets are a constant in an ever-changing world.

- Pets are fun to watch.

- Pets teach children about the living world around them.

- Pets alleviate the hopelessness and helplessness of old age.

- Pets help us remain human and humane.

Alan Beck, ScD, and Aaron Katcher, MD, authors of *Between Pets and People* (A Perigee Book, 1983), cited numerous studies in this book that found that pets, specifically dogs, have a positive effect on their owners' health. But they go on to say, "The studies do not tell us how pets exert this positive effect. It must be by virtue of what they do for people, in some way transforming the lives of their owners."

How Does Bonding Happen?

The bond you establish with your puppy doesn't happen automatically. Although most dogs are born with the ability to bond with people, different breeds and the unique personality of an individual dog affect the level of intimacy they can form with us. As a general rule, the breeds designed to work for people (taking directions and performing tasks) bond more strongly than the breeds developed to work independently.

The best age for bonding with your puppy is 8 to 12 weeks of age. If a puppy doesn't get a chance to interact with people during this time frame, he may never form strong attachments to people. If the puppy has been with other dogs, he may only feel secure with other dogs. If he's been left alone, he may never bond with anyone, human or canine, and will behave more like a wild animal.

The bonding process takes time, patience, and affection. When you bring your puppy home and spend time with him, he will begin to trust you. You need to be kind, gentle, and affectionate, but you also need to begin housetraining and to establish household rules. As you do so, be firm yet fair. Your puppy also needs to respect you. That's part of the process, too.

If you are away from your puppy too much, you leave him alone in the backyard too often, or you are too rough with discipline, then you will forfeit any chance of forming a good bond with your puppy.

The bond will form while you spend time training, playing, caring for, and snuggling with your puppy. You will know you've achieved that bond when you look at your puppy and smile, even if he's just chewed up one of your shoes!

> **"** The best age for bonding with your puppy is 8 to 12 weeks of age. **"**

Miniature Australian Shepherd, 12 weeks old

Maltipoo, 14 weeks old

Women Bonding with Their Dogs

Young animals, including puppies, tend to bring out the maternal instincts in most women. Even if a woman has not had a child, she still tends to treat a puppy with the gentleness, kindness, and caring that she would give a newborn infant.

Women also bond easily in general and researchers feel that this is due to a woman's ability to bond with newborn babies. However, when women transfer this bonding ability to another species such as dogs, the woman and puppy are able to form a strong emotional bond and a wonderful relationship.

Most women enjoy touching their dogs—stroking, petting, grooming, and caring for a dog. Women also enjoy having the dog close by, whether they are doing household chores or simply relaxing. Women are also prone to inviting their dogs to sleep in their beds.

Unfortunately, researchers have found that many women are less likely to establish rules of behavior for their dogs and the nurturing they provide can sometimes turn into spoiling the dog.

Women have told researchers that they own dogs because they enjoy their companionship, they like the feeling of security a dog provides, and they need someone (or something) to care for. When the kids grow up and leave home, a dog often fills that empty nest that's left behind. And many elderly widows add a dog to their lives after the death of their spouse.

Men and Their Dogs

Roy Rogers had his German Shepherd Dog, Bullet, and John Wayne had his Airedale, Duke. In fact, many dogs were cast in movies with John Wayne, several with prominent roles. Men and dogs seem to be made for each other.

Unfortunately, in many regions of the world, including Western cultures, men are also supposed to act tough, unemotional, and sometimes even uncaring. So how does this lead to bonding with a puppy? Luckily, when you present a man with a baby puppy, he forgets what society says he should do and he simply loves the puppy.

Dogs, too, are sensitive to the attention paid to them. Whereas a dog might request more petting and play from his female owner, he knows that his male owner loves him just as much but may express it differently. The dog will not love the male owner any less.

But, thankfully, times are changing and men are demonstrating more emotion even in public. A recent study that observed pet owners in veterinary hospital waiting rooms found that even in a public setting such as this, the men pet their dogs as much as women did with no difference in the type of petting or frequency of petting.

Young men still tend to be rough with puppies—during both play and training—which can lead to the puppy being afraid. Many men enjoy the companionship of dogs as a stress reliever from the pressures of a career. And many elderly men find that a dog can fill an empty spot after retirement.

Miniature Pinscher, 16 weeks old

Chihuahua, 18 weeks old

A Child's Companion

Although experts do not recommend that you make your child solely responsible for a dog, with parental supervision a dog can be a wonderful companion for your child.

Young children are fascinated by puppies and will immediately reach out to touch one. Often the child hugs or strokes the puppy, and when he responds by moving towards the child, he is greeted with delighted squeals and giggles. Young children and puppies bond easily because the children place no pressure on the puppy; they are full of laughter and affection.

Preteens and teenagers find that dogs are wonderful confidants. The puppy listens and offers no judgments, no advice, and no recriminations. The puppy is also a warm, living, breathing entity who loves the child wholeheartedly, which is something the child needs at this age. Puppies form attachments to kids easily, too, as long as they treat the puppy kindly.

> **"Parents need to supervise—closely supervise—all pet relationships with children."**

Unfortunately, adolescent children are sometimes horribly cruel. Sometimes a kid treats the puppy badly because the child feels overwhelmed by life, picked upon, or has been victimized. This misdirected aggression can cause the puppy great emotional and physical pain, and even death. Unfortunately, the puppy cannot tell the parents that the child is treating him badly, so the puppy is vulnerable. In addition, should the puppy bite the child in retaliation, the parents will blame the puppy. Parents need to supervise—closely supervise—all pet relationships with children.

When adolescent children grow up and leave home, many look to pets for companionship. Single people living alone find that a dog is great company as well as a great attention getter when walking or playing in public.

Key Points to Bonding with Your Puppy

Bonding with your puppy is vital to establishing a good relationship with him. The key points to making this work are:

- *The best age for bonding is between 8 and 12 weeks.* However, bonding can happen later as long as your puppy had a good relationship with someone during that time frame.

- *Spend time with your puppy.* Take time to play with him, begin training him, groom him, and snuggle with him.

- *Be gentle and nurturing.* Remember, you are his adoptive mom (or dad).

- *Be firm, yet fair.* Make sure you firmly set the rules for his behavior, but always be fair with him.

- *Don't be rough.* Don't be rough in either your training or your play. Roughness could cause him to fear you or teach him to fight you. Neither is good.

- *Every person in the family can bond with the dog, but each can do so in his or her own way.* Everyone doesn't have to behave the same way with the dog.

Most importantly, enjoy your puppy and the bond you have with him. This relationship is unique in this world.

Jack Russell Terrier, 6 weeks old

Border Collie, 6 weeks old

Chapter 6

**Playing with
Your Puppy**

How Puppies Play

The importance of play in both human and canine lives is tremendous. In children, play helps a child to develop a bond with parents and other kids as well as establish social ties. Play also aids in the cognitive, physical, and emotional well-being of both kids and adults. Puppies benefit from play in many of the same ways.

Puppies begin playing when they're about 4 weeks old. Most play at this age is play fighting. There is growling, biting, shaking, stalking, and wrestling. Things get rough sometimes, but play fighting teaches the puppies how to get along. When one puppy is too rough, the hurt puppy will cry loudly and the puppy who was too rough will back off. The next time she plays, she will temper her bites.

As the puppies grow and develop, toys become important. One puppy will pick up a toy—which can be anything from a leaf to a ball or a rope toy—and she will shake it in her littermate's face, trying to get her littermate to chase her. If her littermate grabs for the toy, the game is on!

Momma dog often instigates play, too. She will pick up a toy and hold it right in front of a puppy, shaking it and making growling sounds. When the puppy grabs the toy, Momma dog may continue to hold the toy while letting the puppy growl, shake the toy, and pull on it. Or she may walk away as she holds the toy, dragging the puppy after her.

Puppies also initiate play by using body language. One puppy may grab a toy and drop it in front of her littermate and then will bow by lowering her front legs and head while leaving her hips and tail upright. All dogs understand that this bowing position is a play invitation.

Australian Shepherd, 20 weeks old

Australian Cattle Dog, 17 weeks old

Using Playtime as a Teaching Tool

Playing with your puppy is good for both of you. Not only will your relationship grow stronger because you and your puppy are spending time together, but the bond you have with your puppy will also strengthen because the two of you are having fun. You're enjoying your time together, laughing, and getting better acquainted. Most play also involves some activity, and exercise is good for everyone.

As you play with your puppy, you'll get to know each other better. You will discover what your puppy's personality is like and how she reacts to things. Does she get angry when she can't have a toy she wants? Does she cry when you play too rough? Do loud noises startle her?

Your puppy will also learn more about you, too. If you're too rough or too loud, then she may worry about you or she may decide to play harder in response. She will figure out what games you like to play. She'll also figure out how to get you to play with her, whether by play bowing to you or by dropping a toy in your lap.

When you play with your puppy, don't let her play too hard. Don't allow her to bite you or any other people she plays with. Although she did use her mouth and teeth when she played with her littermates, you cannot allow this when she plays with people. Unfortunately, today, dogs cannot use their mouths on people; it's considered a dog bite—even in play—and could cause you tremendous legal and financial woes.

You can also incorporate play into your training sessions. Mixing up training and play is absolutely fine. Have your puppy sit and then throw the ball. Have her lie down and then ask her to roll over. It's all good!

The Best Toys

Contrary to popular belief, having a lot of toys is not always best for your puppy. If your puppy has a huge assortment of toys, she may come to the conclusion that everything is hers. This includes your shoes, socks, the kids' toys, and anything else your puppy wants. Instead, you should have a nice selection of toys, but only give the puppy four or five at a time. Then rotate the toys.

For example: On Monday, give her a couple of tennis balls, a KONG toy, a rope toy, and a stuffed duck with a quacking noisemaker inside. On Tuesday, put the KONG toy away and add another rope toy that has a rubber ball on one end. And so forth. This makes your puppy think the toys are new and exciting, and prevents her from believing that everything that she sees, smells, and can fit in her mouth is hers.

"The best toys are those that are hard for your puppy to destroy."

The best toys are those that are hard for your puppy to destroy. Now this will vary from puppy to puppy. Some puppies love stuffed toys and will carry them around in happiness while others try to disembowel them as quickly as they can. It may take some trial and error to discover what types of toys your puppy likes to destroy.

Since you cannot be with your puppy every moment of every day, toys that help keep your puppy occupied are good, too. Many toys are available that you can fill with treats or dry dog-food kibble. Then the treats fall out as the puppy noses the toy around. You can fill KONG toys with treats or a spoonful of peanut butter. This keeps a puppy busy, too.

Border Collie, 8 weeks old

Border Collie, 7 weeks old

Fetch Games

Retrieving games where you throw a toy and your puppy dashes after it, grabs the toy, brings it back to you, and gives it to you are wonderful games. You and your puppy are playing together, your puppy gets some exercise, and you both have fun.

Not all puppies are born with an understanding of this game, although some puppies—especially the retrievers—do seem to know the nuances of this game right away. But even if your puppy doesn't understand right now, you can teach her the fetch game.

Begin by choosing a toy your puppy likes. It may be a tennis ball, another type of ball, or even a stuffed toy. Then sit on the floor with your puppy and bounce the toy around a little so that your puppy looks at the toy. When she pays attention to the toy, praise her by saying, "Yeah! Good toy!"

Then toss the toy just a couple of feet away. When your puppy goes after it, praise her by saying, "Good girl to get the toy! Yeah!" When she picks up the toy, praise her again.

Then call your puppy back by saying, "Puppers, come! Bring me the toy! Yeah, good girl!" When she brings the toy back, offer her a treat in exchange for the toy and tell her, "Give me the toy! Good!"

Remember that the words you use right now to encourage your puppy are the commands you will use throughout her life, so don't use baby talk. Use the words you want her to know, such as "Get the toy" for going after it, "Bring me the toy," and "Give" for offering it to you.

Increase the distance you toss the toy very gradually. Keep the tosses close by so you can encourage and praise your puppy more often.

> " The words you use right now to encourage your puppy are the commands you will use throughout her life. "

The Touch Game

You can play the touch game inside, which is wonderful for those hot, humid summer days or the frigid winter ones. This command, which you can play as a game with your puppy, will also be used later for more games.

Follow these steps to teach your puppy the touch game.

1. Grab a handful of small treats you know your dog likes and put them in your pocket or in a training-treat pouch.

2. Take one treat and hold it in the fingers of your left hand.

3. Open your right hand so your palm is facing away from you.

4. Hold the treat behind your right hand.

5. Gently touch your puppy on the nose with the fingertips of your right hand as you say, "Puppers, touch! Good!"

6. Pop the treat in her mouth immediately.

7. Repeat four or five times and then quit for a while.

With repetition, you will teach your puppy that the touch on her nose by your fingers means the word "touch" and that she also gets a treat. Repeat this game later the same day and then practice two or three times the next day.

Then repeat this exercise, but do not touch her nose with your fingers; stop half an inch away and wait for her to reach her nose forward and touch your fingers herself. Praise her enthusiastically and pop the treat in her mouth. Repeat several times and then do it again later.

Eventually you want to be able to hold your hand out to either side, up or down, and have your puppy move to your hand and touch your fingertips with her nose upon command.

Labrador Retriever, 13 weeks old

Scottish Terrier, 18 weeks old

The Name Game

In the name game, you will teach your puppy the names of several different toys. Once your puppy knows the touch game, then you can either ask her to retrieve the named toy or you can have her touch a particular toy.

Imagine this! You will be able to place five or six different toys in a circle on the floor and then tell your puppy to retrieve or touch one specific toy from among all of them. What a brilliant puppy!

Follow these steps to begin teaching this game to your puppy.

1. Choose one toy that you know your puppy likes.

2. Sit on the floor and toss that one toy just a few feet away.

3. Send your puppy after it and call the toy by name by saying, "Sweetie, get the tennis ball."

4. Praise her with, "Good to get the tennis ball!"

Do this two or three times, stop, and then come back and repeat. After two days of practice, do the following:

1. Place a second toy out in front of you both and toss the tennis ball.

2. Send her after the tennis ball.

3. Praise her when she gets it; ignore her if she gets the other toy instead.

Continue using this technique until your puppy can reliably get the tennis ball every time. Then set the tennis ball aside and start again from the very beginning with a different toy, following all the same steps. If you are patient and follow all the steps, then within several weeks your puppy should be able to identify at least six different toys by name.

Hide-and-Seek

Hide-and-seek is a fun game that uses a puppy's ability to watch movement as well as her scenting ability. This is a great game that kids can play with the puppy. The game requires two people, and you should begin teaching this game in the house.

1. The first person should kneel on the floor with the puppy and hold her collar.

2. The second person should show a dog treat to the puppy, call the puppy's name, and then hide behind a piece of furniture close to the puppy.

3. The first person can say, "Go find!" and encourage the puppy to chase after the second person.

4. When the puppy finds the hiding person, then the second person should give the treat to the puppy and praise her by saying, "Good to find! Yeah!"

After your puppy begins to figure out the game over the next couple of days, then the person hiding can gradually make the game more challenging. He can go to another room, hide in the closet (with the door open), or even hide under a blanket in plain view.

Don't go too far away for quite a while though. For example, leaving your puppy downstairs and hiding upstairs is too much for a young puppy. Don't do that until after you play the game for a few months.

The same goes for playing this game outside. Wait until your puppy is really using her senses well and finds the person in the house every time. Then take the game outside.

English Springer Spaniel

Portuguese Water Dog, 14 weeks old

The Find It Game

In the find it game, your puppy uses her sense of smell to find a hidden treat. This is an easy game that most puppies learn quite quickly. You will need some good treats and something to hide the treat under, such as a small hand towel.

1. Spread the hand towel on the floor.

2. Place a treat on top of it and tell your puppy, "Find the cookie!"

3. When the puppy eats the treat, praise her.

4. Follow these steps a couple of times or until your puppy is excited about going for the treat. Quit for this training session.

For your next training session:

1. Start to fold the hand towel in half, but insert a treat where the fold line begins. Don't drop the top half over the treat because you want your puppy to still see it.

2. Send your puppy after the treat and praise her.

3. Repeat several times, then stop for this training session.

At the next session:

1. Fold the hand towel in half, but this time drop the top half. Then tuck the treat slightly inside the fold so that your puppy can easily find it.

2. Send your puppy after the treat and praise her when she finds it.

Using this same step-by-step technique, you can teach your puppy to find a treat hidden under an inverted small bowl or an empty planter. When your puppy gets good at this game, you can line up three bowls upside down and hide a treat under one bowl. Let your puppy discover which bowl has the treat!

Simple Fun with Household Objects

Play doesn't have to be elaborate; that's one of the joys of playing with your puppy. You can make your play sessions as simple or as complicated as you wish. Teach your puppy to play some of the games you've read about here or make up games as you go along.

Cardboard boxes are great for improvised games. Turn a cardboard box upside down and open one side. Toss a treat inside to encourage your puppy to crawl under the box. Scratch your fingers along the side of the box—making funny noises—so your puppy chases the noises.

Turn the cardboard box right side up and help your puppy climb inside. Fold one of the sides over the top so she can hide in the box. Don't close the top entirely and be careful not to scare her.

Cardboard tubes are fun, too. You can use a paper-towel tube to improvise a noisemaker. Blow through one end and then let your puppy attack the tube. Praise her for being so brave. The tube inside a roll of gift paper is even longer and makes stranger noises when you blow through it.

A sheet of tissue paper wafts on the breeze from a fan and scrunches up well. It makes noises, too, and is great fun for a puppy to chase around on the floor.

As you can see, just about anything is fun for your puppy to play with. Just remember, never give anything to your puppy as a toy that you aren't going to want her to play with later. Once your puppy discovers the fun of cardboard tubes, for example, she's going to remember that! So no shoes, socks, or other clothing, and nothing that can harm the puppy if she chews on it.

English Shepherd, 12 weeks old

Maltipoo, 18 weeks old

Teaching Tricks

Teaching your puppy to perform some simple tricks is fun for you and your puppy, but it is also training. Tricks are a wonderful way to build your training skills and for teaching your puppy that training isn't something that she should avoid.

The goal of all your training—whether it's to play with a cardboard tube, learn house-training skills, listen to obedience commands, or perform tricks—is to develop a working relationship with your puppy so that you can communicate with her and she is compliant to your requests. Because trick training, like play, is fun, it makes training fun, too.

The first trick that many people teach their puppy is to shake a paw. Here's how to do this:

1. Have a handful of treats available.

2. With your puppy sitting in front of you, reach down and tickle the back of her paw in the hollow of her ankle.

3. When she lifts that paw, praise her with, "Good to shake! Yeah!" and pop a treat in her mouth.

4. When you see her begin to lift the paw as you reach for it, touch her lifted paw and praise her. Give her a treat.

5. Then ask her, "Sweetie, shake," and reach for her paw. Praise her when she lifts her paw by herself.

Later you can teach her to shake one paw, then offer the other paw on another command, such as "Other paw!"

Avoid Playing Rough Games

Although people think play is fun and not at all serious, your puppy can take it very seriously. When puppies play, the play is exercise for their bodies, but the games they play also teach them how to get along with other dogs. They learn not to bite too hard, they learn the body language to solicit play, and they learn how to give and take during play.

When you play with your puppy, you're teaching her things about yourself. She learns whether you play gently or rough, whether you're kind and patient, or whether you lose your temper. Hopefully she learns that you play fair and don't take advantage of her youth and inexperience.

But you may be teaching your puppy more than this. If you play rough, wrestle, do tug of war, and allow your puppy to bite—even play biting—you're teaching her that it's okay to fight you and that's a very bad lesson. If your puppy learns to fight people—to use her strength against people—rather than cooperate with people, she could hurt someone and potentially lose her home with you.

Dogs today cannot use their strength and teeth against people. If your puppy bites someone, even in play, the person your dog fights and bites might sue you, animal control could seize and destroy your dog, and you could face criminal charges as well.

Instead of playing rough with your puppy and teaching her to fight people, play games that teach your puppy to be gentle with people and to cooperate with them. A compliant dog is a much safer (and happier) dog.

> **When you play with your puppy, you're teaching her things about yourself.**

Golden Retriever, 9 weeks old

Labrador Retriever, Golden Retriever cross, 3 weeks old

Things Not to Use as Toys

Puppies tend to enjoy certain types of toys more than others. Some like toys that make noise, while others enjoy soft, stuffed toys. Other puppies like balls. It is all a matter of preference. However, what your puppy takes a liking to during puppyhood will tend to remain a favorite as she grows up.

Make sure the toys your puppy plays with are exactly that, toys, and not things the puppy shouldn't have. If your puppy learns to steal socks and then grows to enjoy chewing them up, you may have to fight this sock fetish for the rest of her life. And not only is this annoying and potentially expensive (replacing socks), but many a puppy who likes socks ends up eating one. Removing a sock from a puppy's digestive tract requires major surgery.

> " What your puppy takes a liking to during puppyhood will tend to remain a favorite as she grows up. "

Keep your puppy focused on her toys and not on the family's belongings by puppyproofing your house and yard, as discussed in chapter 1, and by limiting your puppy's freedom, as discussed in chapter 2. Family members also need to remember to put their belongings away. If your son sheds his shoes and socks in the living room as soon as he comes home and then invites the puppy into the room before he falls asleep on the sofa, well, it's not really the puppy's fault if she chews on your son's shoes or socks.

So keep good puppy toys in front of your puppy, put away the things she shouldn't play with, and maintain the puppyproofing of the house and yard that you did when your puppy first came home.

Chapter 7

Socializing Your Puppy

Yorkshire Terriers

The Best Age to Begin Socialization

In order to live with people, a dog needs to accept all the things he sees, hears, and smells in this world. Socialization is the process of teaching your puppy what it's like to live with people. The more things a puppy sees, hears, smells, and feels during early puppyhood, the better able he is to face the challenges he might meet as an adult.

The breeder will handle the puppies from birth so that he can help momma dog care for them, but at 3 weeks of age he begins cuddling the puppies, stroking them, and touching them all over. By the fourth and fifth weeks of life, the breeder and his family will handle the puppies even more. And in the weeks prior to the puppies leaving for their new homes, the breeder will also bring in other gentle people to meet the puppies.

The most important time for socialization, however, occurs after you bring your puppy home. Between 8 to 12 weeks of age, your puppy should meet other people, dogs, and animals, and he should see, smell, and hear the world around him.

Unfortunately, your vet may tell you to keep your puppy at home so he isn't exposed to potential disease. He may recommend that you seclude your puppy until he finishes his vaccinations at 4 to 5 months of age. But this advice ignores your puppy's mental health.

So I recommend a compromise. As you socialize your puppy, stay away from places where dogs congregate, like dog parks, and don't let him sniff the urine and feces of strange dogs, which can pass on many diseases to your dog. Take him to places where he can see people, such as outside schools and shopping centers. Let him meet the older well-behaved, well-vaccinated neighborhood dogs. This way you can socialize your puppy and keep him healthy at the same time.

Australian Shepherd (left), 14 weeks old; and Portuguese Water Dog (right), 13 weeks old

Border Collie (top), 9 months old; and
Pembroke Welsh Corgi (bottom), 16 months old

How to Socialize Your Puppy

You might think that socializing your puppy is easy; just take him with you when you go places and run errands. And that's truc, but socialization involves more than that.

One of the keys to correct socialization is making sure all these introductions are happy experiences for your puppy. Your puppy should feel that meeting people, other dogs, and the park ranger's horse is fun and exciting. If your puppy is afraid when he meets the park ranger's horse, for example, then he may have a fear of horses all his life.

Now some fear is normal. But how you react to his fear is important. Don't try to re-assure your puppy. If he's afraid of a flapping sheet or trash bag, or the park ranger's horse, don't hug your puppy close and tell him, "It's okay, Sweetie, I'll keep you safe." Your puppy isn't going to understand the words, but he will understand that you're holding him close and talking to him in soft tones, both of which he will take as praise for being afraid.

Instead, laugh as you walk him up to the flapping sheet or trash bag and say, "Look at this you silly puppy! This isn't scary!" When you touch it first and encourage him to walk up to it, he can see that fear isn't necessary. Then you can praise him for being brave and pop a treat in his mouth as a reward.

Use this jolly routine for introducing anything new, especially when your puppy appears worried or afraid. Although all of your instincts tell you to protect your puppy, you need to help him stand on all four paws instead.

Sights, Sounds, Smells, and Feels

There are lots of things in the world that your puppy needs to see, hear, smell, and feel. Here are some suggestions.

Make sure your puppy sees:

- Flapping things such as a sheet or a trash bag
- Different things like a sign on the sidewalk, a picnic table at the park, and a fire hydrant
- Household tools being used, including the broom and mop

Your puppy needs to hear:

- Household noises that include the garbage disposal, the vacuum cleaner, the washing machine, and the dryer
- Metal objects, like pots and pans and their lids being clanged together
- The garbage truck coming down the street and a motorcycle zooming past

Smells are important to dogs and are either offensive or attractive to him.

- Car exhaust is not pleasant to either you or your dog, but it's a fact of life. When you go for a walk near traffic, your puppy will smell the exhaust fumes.
- Go for a walk near the beach if you can and let your puppy smell the ocean, the seals, the gulls, and the fish.

Your puppy also needs to feel different surfaces under his paws.

- Walk him on concrete, asphalt, dirt, sand, and on slippery tile.
- Put a plastic bag on the floor and have him walk across that, too.

Border Collie, 13 weeks old

Miniature Australian Shepherd, 12 weeks old

Introducing Your Puppy to a Variety of People

As a dog trainer, I often hear people say, "My dog doesn't like so and so (a certain type of people)." This dislike may stem from the dog owner's personal dislikes or it may be a reflection of a lack of socialization during puppyhood. Puppies who never meet children, for example, may grow up thinking that kids are creatures from another planet. After all, kids don't act like adults, they move faster, have squeaky voices, and do funny things.

Make sure you take the time to socialize your puppy to all kinds of people, including:

- People of all ages, from babies to the elderly and all ages in between

- Kids in strollers, people in wheelchairs, and people using canes or crutches

- People from different ethnic backgrounds

- Short people, tall people, thin people, and heavy people

> **"When introducing your puppy, take advantage of the fact that most people think puppies are cute."**

When introducing your puppy, take advantage of the fact that most people think puppies are cute. You can say, "I'm socializing my puppy, would you like to give him a treat and pet him?" Hand the person a treat and have them feed your puppy. Then have your puppy sit nicely and let the person pet your puppy.

Interrupt the petting if the person gets too rough. Sometimes people like to wrestle with a puppy or tease him, and you should always remove your puppy from those situations. Remember, keep socialization visits happy for your puppy.

Letting Your Puppy Meet Other Dogs

Introducing your puppy to other dogs is tricky; you need to do this wisely. Keep in mind, first of all, that you need to be proactive. Ask the owners if their dogs are fully vaccinated before letting your puppy get close. Since your puppy is still receiving vaccinations, you don't want to expose him to an unvaccinated dog.

Also ask if their dog is patient and tolerant with puppies—not all adult dogs are. A grumpy adult dog could make your puppy afraid of other dogs. In addition, some adult dogs who have never been around puppies or who are impatient may attack your puppy and hurt him severely, both physically and emotionally.

If the adult dog is healthy, vaccinated, and kind with puppies, then let the two greet each other. They will sniff and the puppy may roll over and bare his belly. This behavior is normal; he's being submissive to an adult dog.

If your puppy gets rowdy by bouncing all over and jumping on the adult dog, don't be surprised if the adult dog corrects your puppy. He may growl, bare his teeth, and stand over the puppy. That's OK; don't step in and save your puppy. The adult is just telling the puppy that he's getting too rowdy.

Hopefully, you can also find some puppies for your puppy to play with. In chapter 8, I talk about puppy classes, which are a great way to begin your puppy's training but also enable your puppy to meet a variety of other puppies. Just like kids, puppies need others of the same age to play with.

Labrador Retriever–Golden Retriever cross (left), 5 years old; and German Shepherd Dog (right), 12 weeks old

Visla, 18 weeks old

Cats, Ferrets, Rabbits, Birds, and More

Your puppy is going to share his life with other animals. If you have other pets, perhaps a cat or a rabbit, he's already met them. But throughout his life, he will see other cats and domesticated animals, so you should include them as a part of his socialization.

When he meets these animals, choose ones that you know are friendly. A cat who lives with dogs is ideal, as is a ferret who's familiar with dogs. If they're used to dogs, they are less likely to bite or scratch the puppy unless he gets too rough.

You can introduce rabbits to your puppy, but you also need to protect them. Rabbits can die from fright if your puppy is too rough. But rabbits aren't defenseless, either, and can deliver a powerful kick.

Birds are a little trickier. You can let your puppy see a caged bird or one on a perch, but don't put the two species within grabbing reach of each other.

If possible, let your puppy meet a goat, a cow, a horse, a duck, or even fish in a pond. As with everything concerned with socialization, the more positive experiences your dog can have with other animals, the better.

When you introduce your puppy to any of these animals, make sure he's on a leash so that he doesn't chase them. He should be friendly and calm. Don't allow him to lunge, bark, or chase; if he tries, then turn him away from the animal, put your hands on him, and calm him down. Then let him see the other animal again. When he's calm and curious, praise him.

Going to Different Places and Seeing New Things

The socialization process is a great time to discover (or rediscover) your city. It doesn't matter whether you live in New York City or a rural town; every place has things to see and hear that your puppy has never encountered before.

- Go for a walk downtown so your puppy can hear the cars, trucks, and motorcycles.

- Find a fountain and let your puppy watch the water.

- Walk past overflowing trash cans before the garbage collectors come by.

- Go for a walk past a farmhouse that has goats and chickens grazing on the land.

- Find a shell, a stone, or a rotten log and encourage your puppy to sniff it (but not eat it!).

- Go for a walk in the woods and go off the trail so you and your puppy can discover new things.

- Climb up onto a fallen tree.

- Walk on a low retaining wall.

- Take your dog with you to the hardware store (call ahead to make sure he's welcome inside).

- Bring your puppy with you when you go have a cup of coffee at an outdoor café.

> " Every place has things to see and hear that your puppy has never encountered before. "

Socialization is a wonderful time to rediscover your hometown as well as a great time to bond with your puppy. It's fun, so take the time to enjoy it.

Border Collie, 9 weeks old

Bulldog, 7 weeks old

A Fun Game: Walking on Different Objects

Kate Abbott, who teaches kindergarten puppy classes in Vista, California, sets up a fun socialization game for her students and their puppies. She places a number of different items with different textures on the grass in the training yard. She then has the puppies walk across these items so they can feel these textures under their paws. With their owners' encouragement, the puppies learn they have nothing to fear.

Kate uses:

- A plastic trash bag that she opens up and lays flat
- A tarp with folds and wrinkles in it
- A piece of *hardware cloth* (wire fencing with small squares)
- A piece of corrugated (wavy) plastic
- A piece of plywood with a two-by-four under it so the plywood moves like a teeter-totter
- A child's wading pool with an inch of water in the bottom

To encourage the puppies to walk on these different surfaces, Kate has the owners reach down and touch an item, verbally encourage the puppies, and use a bit of treat as an incentive.

When the puppy walks on each of the items, the owner praises him enthusiastically and gives him a treat. Kate says, "The first time through most puppies are a little hesitant, but the second time around they get braver, and by the third time through they're pros and very proud of themselves!"

Noisemakers Aren't Just for Parties!

Cayla Horn teaches puppy classes and she likes to use a variety of noisemakers to accustom puppies to different sounds. The sounds can be soft, loud, everyday sounds or very different, but she encourages the owners to keep an upbeat attitude during the training no matter what.

Some things that are great for this noisemaking exercise include:

- Dog toys with squeakers inside
- Cat toys that make crunchy sounds
- Kids' toys that make different noises
- Bells of different kinds
- Bicycle bells (the kind that ring)
- Musical instruments, including the harmonica, drums, and tambourines
- Party favors that make noise
- Clickers

As with everything else associated with socialization, you need to act calm and happy when you say, "What's that? Let's go see!" Then praise your puppy for wanting to investigate the sound.

If a puppy reacts with fear to a sound, have him sit, put your hands on him to keep him from trying to run away, and then let him listen to the sound again. Encourage him to walk toward the sound, and when he does, praise him enthusiastically! Don't have the sound come to him; let him walk toward it when he's ready.

Bloodhounds, 12 weeks old

Australian Cattle Dog, 10 weeks old

Don't Overwhelm Your Puppy

Up to this point, I've talked about all the things your puppy needs to experience; now I'll discuss moderation. Moderation in regards to socialization means that you will introduce your puppy to everything he needs to see, hear, smell, and feel, but you will do so in a very gradual process. You've heard of One A Day vitamins? Well, create a one-a-day socialization project. Make it a personal challenge to introduce your puppy to one new thing every day.

- *Monday:* Run the vacuum cleaner while your son or daughter sits with the puppy and talks to him.

- *Tuesday:* Take your puppy to the hardware store and introduce him to the manager, who can give him a treat.

- *Wednesday:* Run the garbage disposal while giving your puppy a treat.

- *Thursday:* Play the harmonica (even if you're not musically inclined) or play some loud music while throwing the ball for your puppy.

- *Friday:* Go for a walk in the woods.

> **"Make it a personal challenge to introduce your puppy to one new thing every day."**

Unfortunately, if you do too much all at once, you can overwhelm your puppy and that could be just as scary to him as not doing any socialization at all. A puppy who feels like too much is happening all at once may shut down; his eyes will glaze over and he'll freeze in place. He just won't move. Or he may panic and try to run away from anything new. So just keep in mind, one a day.

Your Goals for Socialization

A well-socialized dog can cope with the world around him with a minimum of worry. He may startle when a car backfires but then, hey, you may startle at the same sound, too. A dog that startles is OK, but a dog that panics is not.

A well-socialized dog can go places with you. My 4-year-old Australian Shepherd, Bashir, is a well-traveled dog and he handles everything with his normal calm.

Bashir has:

- Been to the Grand Canyon and walked the South Rim

- Been to the hills and rocks of colorful Sedona, Arizona

- Been camping in the mountains of Arizona and California

- Stayed in hotels and motels

- Hiked in the redwood forests of California

- Played on California beaches

- Worked as a therapy dog and gone into nursing homes, hospitals, day-care centers, and libraries

- Ridden in elevators and walked up and down escalators

- Attended dog-training classes of various kinds with many different dogs

- Attended performance dog sports events

- Ridden on a cable car, a bus, a train, and a trolley

All of this begins with carefully planned, gradual, and upbeat socialization of your puppy. Think of this as a foundation for the life you and your puppy will share together.

English Shepherd, 14 weeks old

Chapter 8

Puppy School

You and Your Puppy Both Learn during Training

Training is going to be a normal part of your puppy's life for a long time. Just as children begin their learning early in life and continue through adulthood, so should dogs. In this chapter, you learn how to teach your puppy the basic obedience commands. This training can begin when your puppy is as young as 10 weeks of age. For those who decide to enroll their puppy in a training class instead, I talk about how to find and choose a good class and trainer.

This chapter discusses a training technique that uses your tone of voice, the leash, and food rewards to teach your puppy. This technique is easy to follow for novice dog owners.

Your voice is your most important training tool. You will use your voice to praise your puppy when she does what you ask and when she makes a good decision on her own. To praise her, use a happy tone of voice when saying, "Yeah! Good girl to sit!" You can also use your voice to interrupt bad behavior. If you see your puppy searching through the trash can for buried treasure, use a deep growly voice and say, "Oh no! Get out of there!"

A leash is also a great training tool because it stops your puppy from dashing away when you are trying to work with her. Tiny bits of treats are good for enticing your puppy to do what you ask of her, and they also serve as rewards.

Just as you need to learn how to communicate with your puppy, your puppy needs to learn how to pay attention to you and to accept directions. Because puppies are easily distracted and have short attention spans, training isn't always easy. But the two of you can do it and the end results are well worth the effort.

Rottweiler, 14 weeks old

KINDRED SPIRITS
DOG TRAINING

Congratulations to

Jacques Pierre

For successfully completing a
PUPPY KINDERGARTEN COURSE

Liz Palika * Petra Burke * Kate Abbott

Papillon, 14 weeks old

Choosing a Class and Trainer

If you decide to attend a kindergarten puppy class with your new puppy, do some research first. As I mentioned in the previous section, a variety of training techniques are available, and each trainer who teaches puppy classes has his/her favorite technique. You should choose a class that fits you, your personality, and your puppy best.

Begin your research by calling several local veterinarians and asking which local trainer (or trainers) they recommend. After all, veterinarians see well-trained dogs and not-so-well-trained dogs. The vets also talk to dog owners.

If a neighbor has attended a dog training class, ask if she was happy with that class. If you're out walking your puppy and you see a nicely trained dog walking down the street with her owner, ask where they did their training.

You may find that one trainer's name keeps popping up. That's a strong referral. But once you have one or two names, call and ask if you can come watch a class. Leave your puppy at home and just watch the class. Do the students (humans) look comfortable? Is there a nice balance between lecture and practice? Are the puppies learning something? Would you feel comfortable attending this class?

If your answer is yes, then call the trainer the next day or check out his Web site. Is he certified by one of the national or international dog training organizations? Does he work with all breeds, especially yours? Does he also offer more advanced classes so you can continue to train with him? If all looks wonderful and you feel good about this trainer, then sign up for a class.

Teaching the Sit

Training your puppy will require some self-discipline, especially if you are working on your own at home. However, it's not that hard and can be a lot of fun. If your puppy learns to sit and hold still while you pet her, then she won't jump on people. In chapter 4 you learned how to teach your puppy to sit for petting by using a treat to move her into a sitting position. (See page 107 to review that technique.) However, there is always more than one way to teach a puppy something, so here's an alternative technique. You can try both and see which works best for you and your puppy.

1. Put the leash on your puppy so she can't dash away from you.

2. With the leash in your right hand, place that hand below her chest and neck.

3. As you push gently backwards with your right hand, slide your left hand down her back and over her hips, and then gently fold her back legs under her. At the same time, tell her, "Sweetie, sit."

4. When her hips touch the ground, praise her but keep a hand on her so she doesn't get up on her own.

5. After you praise her, tell her, "Sweetie, OK," and let her get up.

> **There is always more than one way to teach a puppy something.**

Once your puppy understands the sit, you can begin using it. Have your puppy sit before you feed her so she doesn't knock the bowl out of your hands. Have her sit before you let her inside from the backyard so you can wipe off her wet paws. There are lots of ways you can use the sit. Just take a look at your home and your daily routine and then begin asking your puppy to sit.

Bull Terrier, 14 weeks old

Labrador Retriever, 12 weeks old

Teaching the Release

Your puppy actually needs to learn the release command at the same time she learns the sit. The release command lets your puppy know when the exercise is over. For example, when teaching the sit, the exercise begins when you say your puppy's name. That's when you're getting her attention. The release lets her know when she's done and can move and relax for a moment.

When teaching the sit to your puppy, use the words, "Sweetie, OK," to release her. Even though I use "OK" here, you can actually use any phrase you like. Some people say, "Release," while others use "Good job" or "You're done." It's up to you, just make sure you're consistent.

If your puppy doesn't move when you tell her, "OK," then use the leash to encourage her to move or clap your hands as you back away from her. When she gets up, praise her by saying, "Good girl!" With practice she will learn that when you tell her, "Sweetie, OK," it means she's free to move.

If she moves before you give her the release, use your voice to let her know she made a mistake by saying, "Oh no!" and then use your hands to shape her back into the sit. Then when you're ready, release her and praise her.

When teaching your puppy the basic obedience commands, you will use a release with the sit, down, and stay. Because these three commands teach the puppy to hold still—self-control—she also needs to know when she can move, hence a release. If you continue to teach your puppy new things as she grows up, such as tricks, advanced obedience, or even therapy dog work, she will need to know the release command then, too.

Teaching the Down

When you tell your puppy, "Down," you want her to understand this means to lie down. As with the sit, she should not get up until you give her the release command.

1. Begin with your puppy in a sit and hold the leash in your left hand and a treat in your right.

2. Place your left hand (with the leash) on your puppy's shoulders.

3. Let her sniff the treat in your right hand and at the same time move the treat down to her front paws as you tell her, "Sweetie, down." If your puppy has a long body, you may also need to bring the treat forward just a bit to give her room to lie down.

4. When her elbows touch the ground, praise her by saying, "Good to down!" and give her the treat. The left hand should stay on her shoulders just in case she tries to get up.

5. She should hold the position until you tell her, "Sweetie, OK!"

Do not try to do this with your puppy standing; it's much more effective from a sit. After all, her hips are already down in the sit, so all you need to do is lower the front end.

Brittany Spaniel, 12 weeks old

Cattle Dog mix, 12 weeks old

Teaching the Stay

The stay command teaches your puppy to hold the position she's in for a period of time. In basic obedience, you use the stay with the sit and the down, but in advanced obedience you can also use it with the stand.

1. First, put the leash on your puppy and then hold the leash in your left hand. Make sure the leash is not tight. It's not supposed to hold your puppy in position, but rather to restrain your puppy in case she tries to dash away.

2. With your puppy in a sit or a down (your choice), tell your puppy, "Sweetie, stay." At the same time, place your open palm in front of her face for just a second. Don't hold your hand there, just place it and then move it back to you.

3. Don't step away either, just stand by your puppy's side.

4. After five seconds, praise your puppy, pet her, and then release her by saying, "Sweetie, OK."

> "You use the stay with the sit and the down, but you can also use it with the stand."

If she makes a mistake, such as trying to dash away or pull away, or she chews on the leash, just use your voice to calmly say, "No," reposition her in the sit or down, and then repeat the stay exercise.

Over several days you can gradually increase the time your puppy is holding the stay, up to about thirty seconds. Then let the time remain the same, but begin taking a step away from her, working up to going to the end of the leash after a week or two.

Teaching the Come

You want to teach your puppy that the word "Come" means to come to you as fast as possible every single time you call her. To do so, you need to find a really good treat or toy that your puppy really likes. You will use this as her motivator, something that will excite her and help her learn to pay attention to your voice when you call her.

Take a small plastic container, like a margarine container, and put a handful of dry kibble in it. Put the top back on. If you shake it, you will hear a nice rattling sound.

1. With your puppy sitting in front of you, have the shaker in one hand and some good treats in the other.

2. Shake the shaker and then pop a treat in her mouth. You are building an equation in your dog's mind: The sound of the shaker equals a treat.

3. Practice this two or three times and then quit for the first training session, but come back later and do it again.

4. After two or three days of this training, then shake the shaker and say, "Sweetie, come!" and pop a treat in her mouth. Now you're changing the equation. The sound of the shaker equals the word "Come" which equals a treat popped in her mouth!

5. Practice this for several days, two or three times per session. Then start backing away from her as you say, "Sweetie, come!" After a few steps, pop a treat in her mouth and praise her by saying, "Good girl to come!"

With practice, you can slowly increase the distance between you and your puppy when you call her. Praise her and give her a treat every time she comes to you.

Siberian Husky, 15 weeks old

Teaching Your Puppy to Come from a Distance

Teaching your puppy to come with a sound stimulus and a treat teaches her that the come is fun; coming to you results in praise and a treat. That's good! But you also want to teach her to come to you even when she's distracted and would prefer not to come at a given moment.

Hook up a long line—a long leash that is twenty to thirty feet long—to your puppy. You can even use a length of rope if you wish. With the leash in one hand and a treat in the other, back up and call her by saying, "Sweetie, come! Good girl!" When she catches up with you, pop a treat in her mouth. Now, keep the important parts of this exercise in mind when teaching this command:

- The long leash keeps your puppy from dashing away or refusing to come.

- Because your dog is a predator, she thinks that everything that moves is exciting. If you stand still, you're boring. If you move, your puppy is more apt to want to chase you.

- You can also use the leash to keep your puppy from dashing past you, which is a bad habit!

- By giving her the treat when she catches up to you, she learns that you are the giver of good things and coming to you results in a good treat.

As you are teaching the come, make sure you do not use it in your daily routine in a way that will negatively affect your training. Make sure every time you say, "Come," you can actually help your puppy do it. Do not say, "Come," if your puppy is in a situation in which he can easily ignore you.

Havanese, 20 weeks old

Clumber Spaniel, 16 weeks old

Playing the Come Game

The come game continues your puppy's training while making it fun. After all, games aren't work—they're fun to play! Your kids can also play this game with your puppy.

For this game, you need two shakers with kibble in them and two handfuls of good treats.

1. Have two people sit on the floor across the room from each other or at each end of a hallway. Each person needs a shaker and a handful of treats.

2. One person should hold the puppy and then let go when the other person shakes the shaker and calls the puppy.

3. The puppy gets a treat as she reaches the person who is calling her.

4. Then the first person shakes and calls the puppy. The puppy gets another treat if she comes on command.

When the treats are gone, the game is over. But return later and do it again.

When your puppy gets good at this game, then the entire family can sit on the floor, spread out around the room, and take turns calling the puppy. Each person needs to have a shaker and a handful of treats.

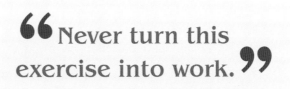

" Never turn this exercise into work. "

Always stop this game, though, before your puppy gets too full or too tired. Remember, you want to teach your puppy that the come is a fun thing to do. Never turn this exercise into work.

Teaching the Watch Me

The watch me command helps to focus your puppy's attention on you. It's almost impossible to teach your puppy if she's distracted by everything else, so teach her to pay attention to you.

Put your puppy on her leash, even if she's in the house with you, so that you can keep her close to you.

1. Hold the leash in one hand and a treat in your other hand. Then let your puppy sniff the treat.

2. As she's sniffing the treat, tell her, "Sweetie, watch me!" and move the treat to your chin.

3. She's going to watch this movement. When her eyes move from the treat to your face, praise her by saying, "Good to watch me!" and pop the treat in her mouth.

Repeat a few times and then take a break. Come back later and do this a few more times. Do *not* do this so many times at one training session that your puppy is too full to take another treat. Just like they say in show business, "Always leave them wanting more!" She's more apt to pay attention to you when you limit the treats.

Do not reward her if she looks away from you. If she gets distracted, she doesn't get a treat. Wait to praise and reward her until you get her looking at your face again.

Now, when you see your puppy come up to you, sit, and then stare at your face, praise her by saying, "Good girl to watch me!" That's what I call a freebie! Praise it!

Labrador Retriever, 13 weeks old

Teaching Your Puppy to Walk on a Leash

You need to teach your puppy to learn how to walk with you without pulling on the leash. Pulling on the leash is very bad on your arm and shoulder, but it can also damage your puppy's neck, shoulders, and chest. Changing to a chest harness doesn't lessen the potential for damage either. Your puppy simply needs to learn to walk without pulling.

1. With your puppy's leash in your left hand and a treat in your right, back away from your puppy.

2. Hold the treat in front of her nose and encourage her to follow you.

3. When she does, tell her, "Sweetie, let's go!" and turn so you are both walking forward together.

4. Praise her by saying, "Good girl!"

5. After a few steps, stop, ask her to sit, and pop the treat in her mouth.

If your puppy gets distracted as you are turning to walk forward together, place the treat in front of her nose to get her attention, then take it up to your face and tell her, "Sweetie, watch me!" Praise her when she focuses her attention on you again.

When she's walking nicely with you, then you can begin to use this technique as you go for a walk. Now, she doesn't need to watch you all the time or focus on a treat all the time, but she shouldn't pull. So when she gets too distracted and forgets you are on the other end of the leash, use this exercise as a training reminder.

Papillon, 14 weeks old

Rottweiler, 14 weeks old

A Socialization Game

In kindergarten puppy classes, socialization is a big part of the curriculum. Puppies get to meet during class and often the instructors will set aside time for play. But meeting other people is important, too, so a game called "pass the puppy" is a staple in many classes.

In this game, all the puppy owners sit on the ground or in chairs in a circle. When the instructor calls, "Pass the puppies," everyone passes their puppy to the left. Each person then snuggles the new puppy, rubs her tummy, and says sweet things to her. After a few moments, the instructor will tell everyone to pass the puppies along again. This pattern continues until the puppies are back with their owners. This game is fun for the puppy owners, who get to meet all the other puppies, but the puppies also meet new people in a sweet, nonthreatening, very positive manner.

You can do the same thing at home. Ask a couple of cooperative neighbors and their kids to come over. Then sit everyone in a circle and pass your puppy around the circle. Everyone gets to pet her for two minutes and then passes her around. Although you pass only one puppy—rather than a whole class—the game is still fun and everyone has a good time.

Another version of this game is spin the bottle. A bottle is on the floor in the middle of the circle of puppy owners. One person spins the bottle and when the bottle stops with the neck pointing to one person, that person gets the puppy. The game continues by spinning the bottle and passing the puppy around. Always stop before the puppy's had enough though. If she's tired or gets grumpy, stop the game.

Puppy Playtime

In puppy classes, time is usually set aside so that the puppies can play together. Letting the puppies chase each other and roll around together is great for many reasons. The puppies get exercise, which is always good, and they continue learning the lessons that began when they were still with their mom and littermates. They learn not to bully, not to bite too hard, and also to give and take.

In the class, the instructor will often explain what's going on to class members so they don't worry that the play is too rough. He may also point out the body language of a puppy who gets too rough or who is worrying. These are all great lessons.

Although you won't have the benefit of an instructor's knowledge at home, you can also set up playtimes if you know someone else with a puppy who is close to the age of your puppy. The puppies need a secure, fenced play area where they won't hurt themselves. They shouldn't be near an unfenced pool or around garden tools that they could knock over. Provide several toys that are sturdy and can stand up to puppy tug of war games.

> **Puppies need a secure, fenced play area where they won't hurt themselves.**

Let the puppies play with as little interference as possible. If one owner tries to save his puppy each time the puppy squeaks or cries, his puppy will never learn how to deal with other dogs. As a general rule, step in and give the puppies a timeout if someone loses her temper or blood is drawn, even accidentally. After a timeout, they can play again.

If a puppy is a bully, then don't invite her back. That puppy might need some help from a dog trainer.

Airedale Terrier

Cairn Terrier, 16 weeks old

Conquering the Confidence Course

Agility is a dog sport that allows dogs to run through tunnels, weave around upright poles, climb obstacles, and leap over jumps of different kinds. Agility is a fast-paced, very athletic sport. Although it's great fun, it's too much for puppies.

Many kindergarten puppy class trainers offer a scaled-down version of an agility course, called a confidence course, for puppies. The puppies learn coordination when they walk or jump over obstacles, and they gain confidence when they succeed at something that may initially frighten them. In addition, the puppies and their owners have fun conquering all these new challenges.

However, you can do the same thing for your puppy at home.

- Take two bricks and a three-foot length of a two-by-four. Place the bricks on the ground about three feet apart and place the two-by-four on top of them. Voila! A jump. Use a bit of a treat to encourage your puppy to jump over the board. Praise her when she does.

- When out on a walk, look for a building with lots of steps in front of it. Walk your puppy up and down the stairs, encouraging her by saying, "Climb! Yeah! Good girl!"

- Find a park that allows dogs and play on the playground equipment with your puppy. Let her walk up stairs, walk across the sway bridge, and slide down the slide. Keep your hands on her, make sure she's safe, use lots of treats, and praise her a lot!

Once you begin looking around, you'll find lots of places where you and your puppy can climb, jump, or crawl. A downed tree, a low retaining wall, and a kid's slide are all potential confidence course obstacles.

Asking Questions about Training Problems

If you have questions about your puppy while raising and training her, ask for help. There are many professionals available—from your veterinarian to a dog trainer to a certified behavioral consultant—who are more than willing to help you.

Here are some common myths about puppies that may answer some of your questions or concerns.

- *Puppies outgrow destructive behavior.* No, they do not. Any behavior that is self-rewarding (such as finding food in the trash can or having fun chewing the stuffing out of a sofa cushion) will continue.

- *Puppies are too young to learn obedience commands; training should not begin until the puppy is 6 months old.* Definitely not true. Puppies are capable of beginning fun, easy training as soon as they join your household.

- *I didn't do [socialization, puppy classes, or (fill in the blank)] with my last dog and she turned out great.* Awesome! You obviously raised her well and she was a good dog. But this puppy isn't that dog, and this puppy might need some more help.

- *Puppies of certain breeds [terriers, hounds, (fill in the blank)] are not trainable.* Wrong! All puppies are trainable.

- *Only problem dogs need to go to dog-training classes.* Nope. Dog-training classes are great places to socialize puppies and to begin their training.

If you have some questions or concerns, ask for help. Don't feel embarrassed; you aren't the first person to ask that question.

Boston Terrier, 7 months old

Welsh Springer Spaniel

Training Takes Time

Building good habits takes time. The behaviors you wish your puppy to know, such as sit for petting instead of jumping on people, takes time. Your puppy needs to sit over and over again before this turns into a habit and becomes an automatic behavior.

It takes time to build new habits in you, too. You need to get into the habit of asking your puppy to sit and to enforce her behaviors, and this takes time.

In addition, your puppy needs time to grow up and become mentally mature enough to think about what she's doing. Right now, as a puppy, she's more apt to react and do things rather than think.

Children begin learning at home, then at preschool, and continue learning throughout kindergarten, elementary school, and on into college. Although your puppy's learning process doesn't have to be quite as formal, it does need to begin early and continue throughout puppyhood and into adulthood.

Keep in mind that for most of our history together, dogs worked for people. Border Collies are still known for being the world's best sheepherding dogs, German Shepherd Dogs have been a versatile working dog breed for a hundred years, and Great Pyrenees are livestock guardian dogs even today. Mankind wasn't rich enough throughout most of history for many dogs to not work for a living.

> "Although many dogs today spend their lives as pets, they still retain the desire and instinct to work."

Although many dogs today spend their lives as pets, they still retain the desire and instinct to work. By beginning training at a young age and continuing the training into adulthood, you build good behavior habits in your puppy and you also give her a job to do. She feels needed, she has something to focus on, and she's less apt to get into trouble.

Chapter 9

Preventing Problem Behaviors

Cattle Dog mix, 11 weeks old

Problem Behaviors Are Not Problems to Your Puppy

Let's face it, puppies can get into trouble. In fact, sometimes your puppy may seem to do nothing but what he shouldn't do! You need to understand that all of the behaviors you consider to be problems—digging, jumping on people, inappropriate and destructive chewing, raiding trash cans, and so on—are not problem behaviors to your puppy. Your puppy isn't doing this to you personally; he's doing it because he's a puppy and doesn't know any better.

- Puppies jump up on people to greet them face to face, just as they would an adult dog. They don't understand that their nails scratch and can hurt people.

- Puppies chew because they're teething and their gums hurt or because chewing on something is fun. What is a shoe to a puppy? A chew toy!

- Puppies bite because they don't have any hands and have to use their mouths to play with their littermates. Puppies have no idea that your skin is fragile or that someone else could sue you if your puppy bites someone.

Many things can affect your puppy's behavior, including what food he eats, how much exercise he gets, and whether or not you have started his training. The relationship you have with your puppy can also affect his behavior, so I'll discuss some important issues you need to think about. And some health problems can cause behavior problems, too, so I'll take a look at when you need to call your veterinarian.

Your goal is to prevent problems from happening as much as possible, and then to teach your puppy alternate behaviors that meet his needs. By doing this, you can eliminate his need or desire to continue most of these problem behaviors. I say *most* because dogs will be dogs and sometimes they will get into trouble.

French Bulldog, 13 weeks old

Nutrition Can Affect Behavior

Many puppies whose diets include mostly foods that have a high glycemic index often show signs of hyperactivity, slow learning, and an inability to retain what they're taught. The *glycemic index* is the speed at which the body converts starches into sugars. Foods with a high glycemic index raise blood-sugar levels very rapidly, providing a quick burst of energy that is followed later by an energy letdown or a crash.

For comparison, here is the glycemic index of several foods:

- Apple: 26
- Barley: 25
- Kidney beans: 27
- Pasta (whole wheat): 37
- Rice (white): 72
- Yam: 51
- Yogurt: 33

Many commercial dog foods, especially dry kibble foods, use rice as one of the primary ingredients. Rice is relatively inexpensive and readily available, and dogs eat it when it's mixed with other foods, especially meats.

However, when puppies eat a diet that has an overall lower glycemic index, they can then focus more readily, learn, and retain what they are taught.

Read the labels on your puppy's food; the first ingredient should be a type of meat such as salmon, beef, chicken, or turkey. Other ingredients can include whole foods such as apples, bananas, sweet potatoes, and other foods that will not send your puppy's blood sugar sky-high. I discuss nutrition in more detail in chapter 10.

Labrador Retriever–Golden Retriever crosses, 7 weeks old

Labrador Retriever, 15 weeks old; Portuguese Water Dog, 13 weeks old; Miniature Australian Shepherd, 15 weeks old; and Australian Shepherd, 22 weeks old

A Tired Puppy
Is a Happy Puppy

Far too few puppies (and adult dogs) get as much exercise as they really need. Without adequate exercise, the puppy can gain too much weight and become chubby (or even fat). He may not develop enough muscle and his bones may not develop as they should. Eventually, this will impact his overall health.

In addition, he may get bored and therefore develop destructive habits. A bored puppy may chew on the lawn furniture, the spa cover, and even the trees in the backyard. Bored puppies often bark too much; run the fence line back and forth and back and forth, potentially developing obsessive-compulsive behaviors; and become escape artists by trying to dig out under the fence, chew their way through the fence, or climb over the fence.

"Ideally, a healthy puppy should have an exercise session three to four times every day."

Ideally, a healthy puppy should have an exercise session three to four times every day. He should run in spurts as he chases a ball or toy, and he can go for a walk with you. He can hunt critters in the woodpile as you cheer him on, or he can play on the agility course at kindergarten puppy class. A puppy alone in the backyard, even a big yard, will not exercise himself enough; he needs encouragement from you and, preferably, your participation.

Do not, however, take a young puppy running with you. The growth plates on your puppy's bones (where new bone forms) do not close until your puppy is from 9 to 14 months old, depending upon his size and breed. He should not perform repetitive motions such as running on hard surfaces for long distances until those growth plates close. If you have questions about this, talk to your veterinarian.

Prevention Is the Name of This Game

If you come home from work and find that your puppy has dug a hole in the middle of your lawn, what do you do? Do you drag him over to the hole and yell at him? Do you whack him with a rolled-up newspaper? Do you put his leash and collar on him and jerk him around? If you do, stop right now. Those things are called corrections after the fact, and they do not work—as you may have noticed.

Puppies (and dogs) live in the moment. If you do nasty things to your puppy when you come home, then your puppy will associate those nasty things with your arrival, not with the digging he did two, four, or six hours ago. Those after-the-fact corrections can potentially damage your relationship with your dog, but will not change any negative behaviors.

Instead, you need to work hard to prevent undesirable behaviors from happening and then you can teach him what to do as an alternative behavior. So, for example, let's look at digging again.

First of all, don't let your puppy dig when you can't supervise him. So keep him in a crate if you're going to be gone a short time. Or if you're going to be gone longer, leave him in a fenced-in dog run or a safe place in the yard where digging isn't a problem. Then, when you're home, supervise him. If you catch him digging, use your voice to interrupt his action by saying, "No dig!" Then redirect him to a toy or a ball and encourage him to play with that instead.

Prevent the problem behavior, interrupt it when it does happen, and teach your dog what to do instead.

Shih Tzu–Bichon Frise mix, 4 months old

Miniature Schnauzer, 16 weeks old

Teaching Your Puppy How to Be Alone

Simon, a Rhodesian Ridgeback, joined his new family when he was 8 weeks old. The timing just happened to coincide with the beginning of summer vacation from school. Mom, who taught school, was home for the next twelve weeks as were all three kids in the family. Simon had a great summer, but he was left alone every day when Labor Day came around and everyone went back to school. He barked, chewed on the plants in the backyard, and dug holes in the lawn. He chewed up the garden hose and pulled the television cable out of the side of the house.

Although Simon caused a great deal of damage, upset the neighbors, and horrified his owners, it wasn't his entire fault. As far as Simon was concerned, he had been abandoned. He was used to having people with him. And when everyone disappeared, he was frightened, bored, and lonely.

Your puppy needs to learn to be comfortable when he's left alone. Begin by putting him in his crate (or a safe place outside) with a toy or biscuit and then walking away. Let him remain in the crate for half an hour or so, then let him out if he's quiet. Never let him out if he's barking, crying, or throwing a temper tantrum. Gradually increase the time he stays alone.

You can slow down any destructive tendencies by leaving him in a place where you have put away or picked up anything he can destroy. Always leave him with an appealing toy or chew toy, and put on some easy-listening music nearby. Make sure, too, that he gets exercise before you leave him each day.

Being a Leader to Your Puppy

For many years, pet experts encouraged dog owners to assume the role of their puppy's pack leader as they raised their puppy. Puppy owners were told that pack leaders are tough disciplinarians and expect puppies to toe the line or else!

As you've read elsewhere in this book, being your puppy's parent is a much more reasonable position. You understand the job parents are expected to do when raising babies (humans or puppies), and most people feel more comfortable being a parent than being a pack leader.

However, parents are leaders, too, and your puppy needs you to be his leader, especially as he moves from puppyhood into adolescence and on into adulthood. But don't worry; being a leader isn't hard and much of it is common sense.

- Ask your puppy to wait and follow you through doors and gates. This is common courtesy; he shouldn't dash through doors ahead of you. He could end up outside in the street or he could trip you.

- Practice your basic training commands and make sure your puppy does them. Don't make excuses like, "Oh he's tired today." Make sure he will sit for you, lie down, stay, and follow you nicely on the leash.

- Establish and enforce your household rules. Make sure all family members do the same.

- Do not tolerate rude behavior. If he growls at you, snaps, or worse yet, lifts his leg to urinate on your belongings (or you!), call a dog trainer for help.

Boxer, 16 weeks old

Border Terrier

Teaching No Bite!

As mentioned earlier in this book, a puppy uses his mouth to play bite his littermates, manipulate his toys, and discover his world. Puppies don't have hands, so everything goes in their mouths.

When your puppy was with his mother and littermates, they taught him to be careful when he bit them. If he was too rough during play, a littermate would yip and cry; momma dog might correct him; and the littermate wouldn't play with him.

People have a tendency to be much too tolerant of puppy bites. They make excuses, such as "He's just a baby and he'll grow out of it!" That's not true at all and is potentially dangerous. Your puppy needs to learn right away that he's not allowed to use his mouth on people at all—ever!—because dogs who bite people are dangerous.

So, if your puppy uses his mouth on you during play, accidentally or otherwise, you should say, "No bite!" and immediately stop playing. Have your puppy go to his crate or outside, or you go inside. You have to be just this short, sharp, and curt to make an impression. In half an hour, bring him back and begin playing again.

If he uses his mouth while you're grooming him, checking his ears or teeth, or are otherwise taking care of him, use your finger and thumb to close his mouth as you tell him, "No bite!" You are not being rough, you are closing his mouth to show him what "no bite" means.

> **"Your puppy needs to learn right away that he's not allowed to use his mouth on people at all—ever!"**

Now if he makes a good decision, perhaps he turns his mouth towards your hand but stops, then praise him by saying, "Good boy!" Let him know you appreciate this behavior.

What Is Aggressive Behavior?

Some puppies are born with aggressive instincts, especially those bred as working dogs, guard dogs, or protection dogs. German Shepherd Dogs, Belgian Malinois, Cane Corso, and other breeds designed to protect people and property may eventually show aggressive tendencies.

Although the term aggression has come to have a bad reputation, it isn't always a bad thing. Many people want a dog to bark and growl when someone tries to enter their property. Others may want a dog to protect their car or home. Your dog should never show aggression toward you or your family, however, and you must always be able to tell your dog to stop.

When puppies are with their littermates, they will play fight and they will bite each other, growl, snarl, and sound positively fierce with their high-pitched puppy voices. Once your puppy comes home with you, don't allow him to transfer that play fighting to people. Your puppy should never fight you (play or otherwise) and should he do so, immediately stop him by saying, "Oh no! I can't believe you did that to me! How rude!" Then put your puppy in his crate for a timeout until he calms down.

You must stop this aggressive behavior right away, without fighting him or reacting in any other way, because it is rude for him to do it. His mother would never allow him to be rude to her. In addition, he should never get the idea that this is acceptable behavior.

This also means that no one in your family should play wrestle with your puppy. That's teaching him to fight people, which is exactly what you are teaching him not to do!

German Shepherd Dog, 12 weeks old

Rhodesian Ridgebacks

Resource Guarding Might Require Professional Help

Another potentially aggressive behavior is when a puppy begins guarding things that he thinks are special. Some puppies will growl if anyone approaches while they are eating, while others will hide and protect special bones or toys. This behavior is called resource guarding.

Although a certain amount of resource guarding is natural—your puppy may hide a bone and then sit on top of it—you should never allow your puppy to growl, snarl, or snap at people. Nor should your puppy feel that he has to protect everything.

Some puppy owners try to make sure that resource guarding doesn't get established by reaching into their puppy's food bowl while he's eating. The theory is that this teaches the puppy that his owner has the right to take his food. Unfortunately, this does just the opposite in far too many cases. The puppy seems to think, "Oh my gosh, they're reaching into my bowl again! They're going to take my food again! I have to protect my food!"

A better way to prevent resource guarding is to trade one thing for another. Have a good toy, use it when you play with your puppy, and then ask him to bring it to you. Offer him a good treat for the toy, trade, and then praise him by saying, "Thank you for giving me your toy! Good boy!" and then repeat the game again. This method teaches him that you will trade one good thing for another, that you are happy when he gives you the toy, and that he's a good puppy when he shares.

If at any time, though, you feel that your puppy is becoming aggressive about guarding his food or toys, call a trainer or behaviorist for professional help. If you ever get the feeling your puppy may bite, then call for help.

Teaching Your Puppy Not to Jump on People

A puppy greets his mother and other adult dogs by jumping up and licking the adult dog's muzzle. Puppies like to lick people's faces for the same reason. Unfortunately, when your puppy jumps on you he can get you all dirty or muddy, rip your clothes, scratch your skin, and knock you down. So even though your puppy doesn't mean to hurt you when he jumps on you, you need to teach him not to jump up.

When you taught your puppy to sit for petting (first in chapter 4 and again in chapter 8), you taught him what pet experts call an alternative behavior. Your puppy cannot jump on people to greet them if he's sitting. So, when he learned to sit for petting, he learned an alternative behavior.

However, sometimes your puppy will be just too excited to hold still and he'll need some help to sit. There are a couple different techniques you can use.

> **"Sometimes your puppy will be just too excited to hold still and he'll need some help to sit."**

First of all, when you come home and your puppy is excited to see you, greet him with empty hands. Put down your purse or briefcase and leave the groceries in the car for a few more minutes. As your puppy jumps up, grab his collar with both hands and tell him, "Sweetie, no jump! Sit!" and with one hand remaining on his collar, use the other hand to shape him into a sitting position. Keep your hands on him because he's apt to jump back up. Praise him while he's sitting.

Don't ask your guests to do this with your puppy because they won't do it consistently. Instead, when your puppy is going to greet other people, put his leash on him and you can help him sit. Don't let people pet him until he's sitting.

Puggle, 20 weeks old

Jack Russell Terrier, 16 weeks old

Teaching Your Puppy to Sit at Doorways

Dashing through every door is dangerous for your puppy. Your puppy could dart through the front door and end up in the street where a car could hit him. In the house, dashing through doorways is rude; he could knock you down.

Instead, teach your puppy to be safe as well as polite. He should wait at doors for permission to go through them and then calmly follow you through all doorways, inside and out. Follow these steps to teach your puppy to wait at doors.

1. Put your puppy on his leash so he can't dash away.

2. Walk to a door—any door in the house—and close it.

3. Sit your puppy at your side as you face the door. Tell your puppy, "Sweetie, wait."

4. Praise him for sitting and then open the door. If your puppy dashes through the door, use the leash to stop him and bring him back to your side as you tell him, "No, I said wait."

5. Close the door again and repeat the exercise.

After a few repetitions, take a break and come back later and repeat this exercise. When he's no longer dashing through the door, repeat the exercise at other doors in the house.

When he's got the idea, take the exercise a step further. Sit him by your side, tell him "Wait," open the door, and then step through the doorway. If he moves, tell him, "No! I said wait!" and put him back where he began. Repeat the exercise. Practice this at all doors in the house, as well as the gate, the garage door, and other openings to the outside world.

To make this work, you must always have your puppy sit at doorways. Then give him permission to go through. If you don't make him sit at doorways consistently, then your puppy won't be reliable.

Barking Can Quickly Become a Neighborhood Problem

You've probably already figured out what sounds your puppy makes for certain things: his cry when he's hungry, his bark when someone comes to the door, and his play bark.

Some dogs, unfortunately, can take barking too far. They may decide it's important to bark every time they hear a siren. If you live near a busy street, this is a huge problem. Some dogs want to bark at every person who walks by the house or at the mail carrier's truck and the UPS truck.

Some breeds are more prone to barking than others: Dachshunds, German Shepherd Dogs, Cocker Spaniels, and Australian Shepherds are all typically bad barkers, but they certainly are not alone. Just about any dog can be a barker.

When a dog decides to bark too much, neighbors will quickly become angry. Barking can disturb sleep, hamper concentration, bother someone who is ill or recuperating, and make a baby fussy.

When you're at home, stop all barking immediately by firmly saying, "No! Quiet!" and follow through by stopping it. Never allow your puppy to ignore you and continue barking. If you have to, go outside with a squirt bottle and spray the water mist towards the puppy as you tell him to be quiet.

Then one day go through all the motions like you're leaving the house. Get dressed, get your keys, and drive the car down the block. Then walk back and sit outside your house with a squirt bottle in hand and as soon as your puppy barks, squirt over or through the fence and say, "*No!* Quiet!"

Also, if your puppy is prone to barking too much, then make sure he get lots of exercise prior to leaving him alone. A tired puppy is more apt to take a nap rather than bark!

Cairn Terrier, 13 weeks old

Bloodhounds, 6 weeks old

Destructive Chewing Is Dangerous

Puppies chew on things for many reasons. They usually begin chewing when they are teething; the teeth are coming in and the gums hurt. Puppies also chew when they're bored and haven't had enough exercise, but they also chew because it's fun. As you know, puppies will continue to do anything that is self-rewarding and having fun certainly is self-rewarding.

But your puppy's chewing is expensive when he damages your things and you have to purchase replacement items. Plus, chewing is dangerous. Swallowing some bits of plastic, your dirty sock, or other items can potentially threaten his life.

You can handle destructive chewing from four different approaches, and with most puppies you will need to use all four techniques.

1. Practice prevention. Put things away, especially anything that your puppy shows interest in. That means putting the television remote control out of your puppy's reach and having everyone put their clothes away. Keep cupboard doors closed. Just think prevention.

2. Then limit your puppy's freedom. If he's not running loose in the house unsupervised, then he will have a much more difficult time finding things to chew on.

3. Give him something that he can chew on and praise him when he does chew on it. If he shows interest in something you don't want him to chew, then hand him his chew toy.

4. When you do catch him with something in his mouth that he shouldn't have (and only then) interrupt him by saying, "Oh no! That's not yours!" and take it away. Then take him to his chew toy and encourage him to chew on that instead.

Do not assume that your puppy will outgrow this chewing problem, because he won't! Puppies do not outgrow self-rewarding behaviors. You need to take action on this.

Teaching Your Puppy to Stay off the Furniture

It's up to you whether you want your puppy on the furniture. You can give him one piece; you can allow him on all the furniture; or you can teach him to stay off all the furniture.

However, think carefully about it now because changing the rules later is very difficult. If you have an old sofa now and don't mind your puppy lying on it, but you plan to keep him off the new sofa that you'll purchase soon, then don't let him up on the old sofa now. He won't understand the change in the rules later.

To teach your puppy to stay off the furniture, simply don't let him up on it. In addition, don't leave him alone in the house unrestricted because that gives him every opportunity to sneak up on the couch. Instead, leave him in his crate or in a safe place outside.

Consistency is important in teaching this behavior. Don't allow your puppy up sometimes and scold him for climbing up at other times. He doesn't understand that the reason he can't come up is because his paws are wet or he's been rolling in the mud. You have to be consistent.

> **"Changing the rules later is very difficult."**

Family members have to enforce the rules regularly, too. If Mom and Dad enforce the rules but the kids sneak the puppy up when their parents aren't looking, this will confuse the puppy and he will try to keep coming up on the sofa.

Cairn Terrier, 12 weeks old

Beagle, 12 weeks old

Preventing Begging

Begging is a very annoying behavior. Not only is it hard to enjoy your meal when two dark brown eyes watch your every move, but begging can quickly escalate into worse behavior. Some dogs will paw at your leg or arm if you don't feed them when they beg, and they might scratch you with their sharp claws. Other dogs begin stealing food, both from the table and from the kitchen counters.

The easiest way to prevent begging is to never feed your puppy from your plate. Don't share bits of food with him no matter how cute he is or how prettily he begs! And don't let other family members share either.

If you wish to let your puppy have some of your leftover food, fine, just give it to him in his bowl at his mealtime. Or let him work for some treats away from the table after you finish eating. Ask him to sit for a bit of food and then lie down for another. Teach him some tricks so he can earn a few more treats.

If your puppy is already begging under the table, the best way to stop it is to teach him an alternative behavior. Teach him to lie down on his bed a short distance from the table. Place his bed far enough away from the table so he can't beg, yet close enough so you can see him and supervise him. When you get ready to go to the table, take your puppy (on a leash and collar) to his bed, ask him to lie down, and then tell him to stay. If he gets up, tell him, "No," and take him back to his bed. When you're done eating, praise him enthusiastically and tell him what a wonderful puppy he is!

Are You Causing Your Puppy's Behavior Problems?

Puppy owners often cause behavior problems (or make them worse) without realizing it. If you aren't meeting your puppy's needs of exercise, good food, or time for play, then he may respond by doing things you wish he wouldn't do. But you may affect your puppy's actions in other ways, too.

Many owners think that their job as a parent means they need to protect their puppy. Yes, you should protect your puppy from obvious harm, but if you overprotect him, then he will never learn how to function with other puppies or people and will never learn how to cope with the world around him.

Overly permissive owners often feel that you should allow puppies to do as they wish. Although this sounds wonderful, in practice it's wrong. Puppies need to learn the rules that they will have to live with throughout their lives. Dogs who aren't taught this as puppies have a very tough adjustment to make later, which isn't fair.

The very best thing that you can do for your puppy is to be a steady, stable, fair, and humane owner.

- Establish some rules for behavior and then enforce those rules consistently.

- Praise good behavior and interrupt or prevent bad behavior.

- Practice your puppy's training often, show your puppy what you want him to do, and praise him well when he cooperates.

Puppies don't try to be bad; they just need to learn what you expect of them. Then they are usually happy to comply.

Basset Hound

243

Pug, 16 weeks old

Health Challenges Can Cause Behavior Problems

Experts in the field of canine behavior say that fully 20 percent of all behavior problems may be related to the dog's health.

- If your puppy is doing well with his housetraining but begins urinating in the house, then he may have a urinary tract infection.

- If your puppy is doing well in his housetraining but then has fecal accidents in the house, he may have an upset stomach or other gastrointestinal upsets.

- Intestinal worms may also cause fecal accidents in the house.

- A puppy who is chewing on everything he can fit into his mouth may be teething.

In addition, many medications can cause behavior changes. Steroids, which are given for many different medical conditions, can cause a dog to drink more water and urinate more often than normal, which could cause housetraining accidents. Steroids can also make your dog grumpy.

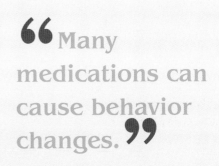

"Many medications can cause behavior changes."

Make sure you talk to your veterinarian about any behavior that you suspect may be caused by a health problem. Don't just take your puppy to the vet and ask, "Is he OK?" Instead, ask specific questions and give as much information as possible such as, "Sweetie has been doing very well in his housetraining, but yesterday and today I noticed several accidents in the house. It also seems like he's urinating more than usual. Do you think there might be a problem?"

If your veterinarian prescribes any medications, always ask what side effects you should watch for, both physically and behaviorally.

Labrador Retriever

Spaniel mix, 18 weeks old

Choosing Your Puppy's Healthcare Partner

Your puppy cannot care for herself. Oh, she may lick her paw should she get a scratch on a pad. But she cannot pull tangles out of her coat or get rid of fleas. She needs your knowledge and assistance to maintain her good health.

Your puppy's healthcare begins with her veterinarian, who is your partner in your puppy's healthcare. You can find a good vet in your area by asking pet-owning friends where they take their pets. Are they happy with this vet? Are his prices fair? Is his staff helpful? Once you have a vet or two via recommendations, make an appointment (without your puppy) so you can ask him some questions. (Be prepared to pay for his time.)

- First of all, is he comfortable with and knowledgeable of your puppy's breed? Not all vets like German Shepherd Dogs, Pit Bulls, or Chihuahuas, for example.

- What are his policies concerning emergencies? Know his policies before you have an emergency.

- Is he flexible in his approach to medicine? You may want to use some alternative remedies, such as herbs or acupuncture. If you have some preferences, is he willing to listen?

- What credit cards does he accept? This is important, especially during an emergency.

Once you find a veterinarian you like, take your puppy in for an examination and to set up a shot schedule. Ideally, this should happen during your puppy's first week with you and certainly no later than her second week as your puppy will need vaccinations so that you can begin socialization. During the initial visit, the vet will examine your puppy, checking for any health problems, and will start her on vaccinations. Bring any health records you may have for your puppy, including any vaccinations the breeder may have given the puppy.

Labrador Retriever, 5 weeks old

Feeding Your Puppy a Nutritious Diet

In chapter 9, I discussed nutrition in relation to puppy behavior. You know that you should base your puppy's food on meat products and that carbohydrates should ideally come from low glycemic foods such as sweet potatoes and apples, rather than high glycemic foods like rice or other cereal grains.

But even with this information in mind, you may find it hard to choose a good food. There are a lot of commercial dog foods to choose from.

- *Dry kibble foods:* These are dry and crunchy, easy to serve, and range in price from cheap to more expensive, usually dependent upon the quality of ingredients.

- *Canned foods:* These are meat or meat recipes packed in water. Compared to dry foods, these are quite expensive.

- *Raw foods:* Raw meat, vegetables, and fruits are offered to your dog. You can find commercially prepared diets that are frozen or you can feed your dog from a recipe at home.

There are other options, too. Dehydrated foods are commercially prepared raw-food diets that have the benefits of raw foods (uncooked nutrients) with the safety of dehydration. Plus, many people like to feed their dog the same foods they feed their family.

The best thing you can do for your puppy in regard to food is to become an educated consumer. Understand the labels and the ingredients list. Then choose a food that you feel comfortable with, one that has good ingredients and that you can afford to feed your puppy over a period of time.

When and How to Feed Your Puppy

Feeding your puppy involves much more than filling a bowl with dry dog food and setting it on the porch in the backyard so your puppy can pick at it all day. No, although this method is convenient, it's not the best way to feed your puppy.

First of all, she needs scheduled mealtimes. She will need to relieve herself after eating, so she needs to practice her housetraining skills on a regular schedule, too. If she nibbles at her food all day, you won't know when she needs to go outside.

Also, should she not feel good, one of the first things the veterinarian will ask is, "How is her appetite?" If your puppy eats a bite here and there, then you can't answer that question.

Most puppies need to eat twice a day although many small-breed puppies may even need three meals per day. If you have questions, ask your veterinarian.

Feed your puppy in a quiet place where no one can disturb her. In her crate is fine. Don't mess with her food and make sure the kids leave her alone. If you have other pets, feed each one separately and don't let anyone steal her food.

Give her the bowl and when she's done, take the bowl away. If she stops eating but some food is left-over, take it away. Don't leave it out; leftover food will attract ants, flies, or other critters.

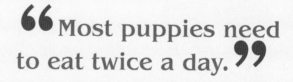

66 Most puppies need to eat twice a day. 99

Last but certainly not least, feeding your puppy is an important part of your relationship. When you give your puppy her meals twice a day, then you can cement in her mind that you are the giver of her food. In her world, that's huge!

Labrador Retriever, 15 weeks old

Miniature Australian Shepherd, 12 weeks old

The Daily Massage

Giving your puppy a massage every day is a wonderful routine to establish. Not only will both of you enjoy this, but your puppy learns that you can touch her all over and you won't hurt her. This will help tremendously during your daily grooming sessions as well as when you need to care for her when she's hurt or sick.

To begin the massage:

1. Sit on the floor and invite your puppy up on your lap or between your legs.

2. Turn her paws away from you so she can't scratch you.

3. Begin at her head and gently investigate her entire head by using a soft touch. Check out her ears, touch her eyelids, and look at her teeth.

4. Then massage behind the ears, down the neck, and into the shoulders.

5. Massage each front leg and then feel between each pad of each foot, touching the toenails, too.

6. Gently massage her entire body and then work down the back legs and her tail.

You want to touch every inch of her body so that she learns to accept the handling. In addition, you will learn what her body feels like so you can detect when there is a problem, such as a lump or bump or burr in the coat.

Try to massage your puppy once a day. Not only does it enhance your relationship and teach your puppy to trust you, but it also helps you find and take care of any bumps and scratches on her. After all, puppies are notoriously clumsy.

Brushing, Combing, and Removing Tangles

Your puppy needs regular combing and brushing to keep her coat clean and neat. Brush shorthaired dogs, such as Boxers and Doberman Pinschers, with a soft-bristled brush. The soft bristles won't scratch the skin. Medium- and longer-coated dogs need bristles that go all the way through the coat. At least two or three times per week, brush your puppy thoroughly, making sure you get behind the ears, on the belly, and behind the back legs as well as the body.

A comb can help work out tangles (also called mats) that form in the coat. If a tangle is tough to comb through, gently work a little cornstarch into the hairs with your fingers and then try to pull them apart. Never try to cut a mat out; the skin pulls up easily under the matt, and you will cut the skin as well as the hair.

If you bought your puppy from a breeder, she can guide you as to the grooming requirements of your puppy. Many breeds have special needs. For example, you need to hand strip many terriers for a proper coat. Hand stripping, which is the process of pulling the dead hairs out of the coat, takes some special skills and lots of practice to do correctly. Other breeds, including Poodles and Cocker Spaniels, usually go to a professional groomer every four to six weeks for brushing, bathing, and trimming.

Even if you don't have a Poodle or Cocker Spaniel, a professional groomer can assist you. He can show you a variety of tools you can use, including combs, brushes, toenail clippers, and more. To find a groomer, ask for a referral from a friend or neighbor who takes her dog to a groomer.

Portuguese Water Dog,
15 weeks old

Golden Retriever–Labrador Retriever cross, 8 weeks old

Bathing Your Puppy

Once you thoroughly brush your puppy and all the tangles are out of her coat, you can bathe her. Before you begin, gather your supplies. You will need a couple of towels, some shampoo and conditioner that is safe for puppies (read the label), a couple of cotton balls, and a handful of treats. (Give her treats now and then throughout the process.)

You can bathe your puppy in the tub or if she's tiny, in the sink. Test the water to make sure it's warm but not hot. Lift your puppy into the tub and keep one hand on her at all times so she cannot jump out. Put a cotton ball in each ear to help keep her ears dry.

" Test the water to make sure it's warm but not hot. "

Using a handheld sprayer, wet your puppy. When she's wet all over, begin working the shampoo into her coat. Start at her head and work back towards her tail and then down each leg. After you cover her in shampoo, give her a good scrubbing to loosen any dead hair and all the dirt. Then rinse well. After all the shampoo is out, follow the instructions for using the conditioner and then rinse it out well.

Wrap your puppy in a towel and lift her out of the tub. Dry her off as best you can, switching towels if one gets too wet. If the air temperature is OK, let her air-dry. If it's cool, use a hair-dryer to dry her more quickly. Just make sure the temperature on the blow-dryer is cool enough so she doesn't overheat or get burned.

Once she is dry, brush her again to remove all the loosened dead hair and comb her to make sure she has no tangles.

Fleas, Ticks, and Mites

Fleas, ticks, and mites are parasites that live on the outside of your puppy's body. These external parasites feed off your puppy and carry some dangerous diseases.

Fleas are tiny, crescent-shaped insects with flat sides that move easily through a puppy's coat. They bite the puppy for a drop of blood to feed on, but they drop off the puppy to lay eggs in the carpet or in the dirt outside. If you see one flea, at least a hundred more are on the puppy or in the environment.

Ticks are eight-legged insects that bite a puppy and then feed on the blood until they are full. Then they drop off the puppy to lay their eggs. To remove a tick, grab it with a pair of tweezers and gently twist and pull.

To control fleas and ticks:

- *On your puppy:* Your vet can recommend products that you either drop on your puppy's skin or have your puppy ingest. These products work systemically in the puppy's body and either kill the insects or make them unable to reproduce.

- *In your home:* If you find you have fleas or ticks in the house, spray the entire environment with a flea spray. Buy a product that is safe to use around puppies and use it according to directions. Then vacuum the entire house and wash all the bedding where the puppy rests and sleeps, including your own.

- *In the yard:* Again, just as in the house, use a product (usually a spray, but some granules are available) that is safe to use around puppies.

Demodectic mites can cause small bald spots on a puppy, and although these spots do not itch, they require veterinary treatment. **Sarcoptic mites** cause itchy spots that the puppy will continually try to scratch. This, too, requires veterinary treatment. Sarcoptic mites can be transmitted to people.

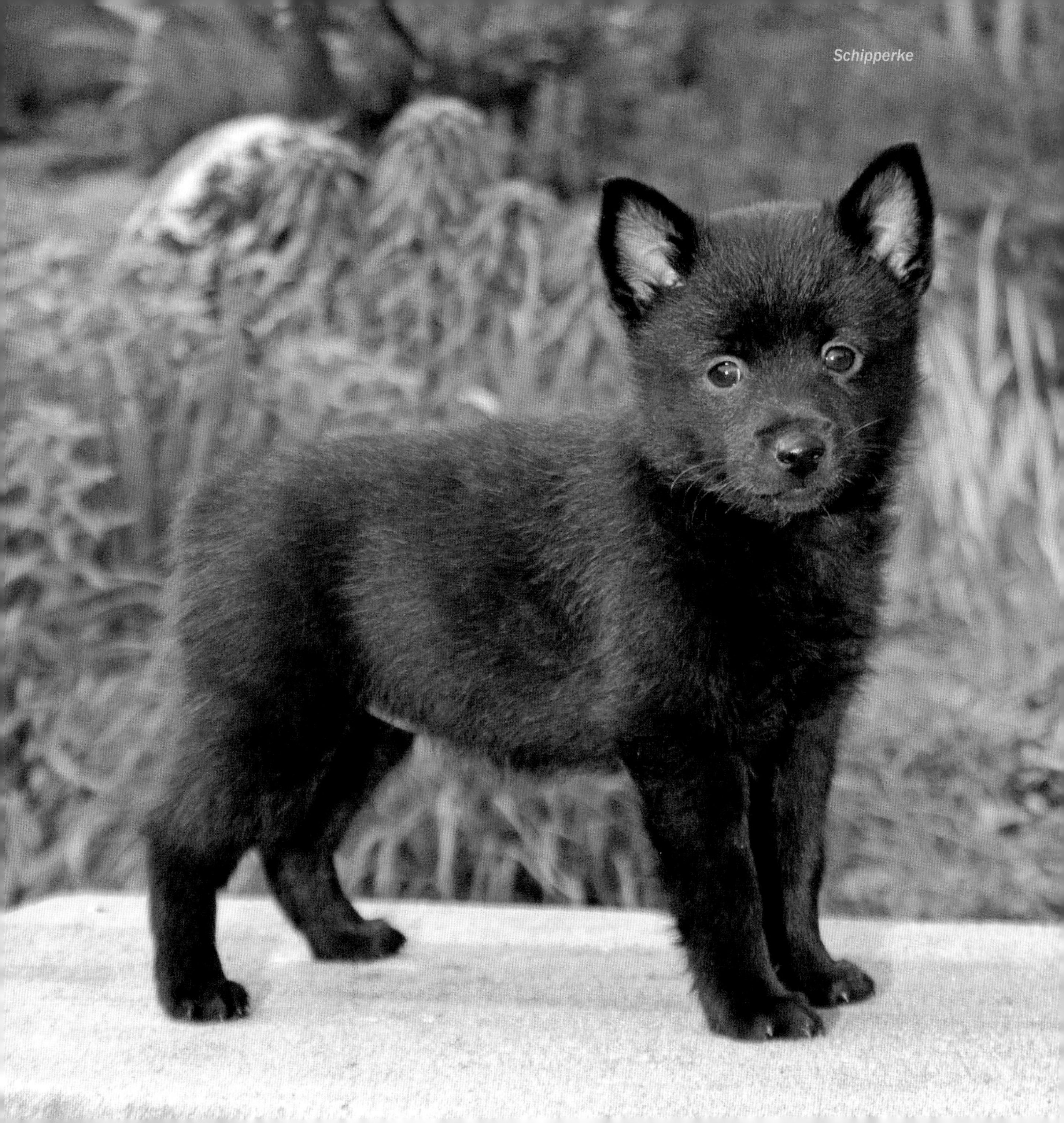
Schipperke

Boxer, 14 weeks old

Cleaning the Eyes, Ears, and Teeth

Healthy eyes are easy to care for; once a day just wipe a damp paper towel over the eyelids to remove any dirt or crustiness. However, if your puppy produces excess tears, the hair around the eyes might remain damp, which can cause problems. Use an anti-bacterial wipe (the kind made for people is fine) and gently clean the areas around and under the eyes. Then dry the hair with a towel.

When you brush your puppy, dampen a cotton ball or pad with either witch hazel or an ear-cleaning solution to wipe out your puppy's ears. To do this, fold the earflap over your puppy's head and then gently wipe the inside of the earflap and the areas of the ear you can most easily reach. Do not try to go farther into the ear.

Get into the habit of checking your puppy's ears regularly. Once per week is a minimum, but daily is better. If your puppy gets water in her ears, or a grass seed or other foreign object, an infection can develop rapidly. These are very painful and require immediate veterinary care.

Although your puppy will lose her baby teeth and get new ones, you still want her to learn how to accept tooth care. It's much easier if you begin when she's a baby puppy rather than try and introduce it later when she's older.

Make a paste of baking soda and water, about the consistency of toothpaste, and using a child's toothbrush, begin gently brushing your puppy's teeth. It's not easy to do this; her tongue will continually get in the way, but don't give up. Get into the habit of brushing her teeth daily.

Teething Problems

Puppies begin *teething*—losing the baby teeth and growing in adult teeth—between 4 and 5 months of age. The first teeth to disappear are usually the tiny front teeth on the top and bottom jaws at the front of the mouth. You may see a bit of blood on the gums, but people rarely find these teeth; they usually just disappear. However, when the larger teeth fall out—the big canines or molars—these are often found on the floor. Often by bare feet!

When the adult teeth are growing in, the puppy can go through many of the same problems human babies have when they are teething. The puppy may be grumpy, lose her appetite, run a fever, and have red and swollen gums. She may chew voraciously because that will make her gums feel better. Offer lots of chew toys so she always has something to chew on. Ice is good, too, because it can deaden the pain for a few moments.

Here is a good recipe for teething puppies:

Chicken Cubes

½ cup chicken, cooked and finely shredded

1 cup chicken broth

1. Put cupcake paper liners in six cupcake forms of a cupcake or muffin pan.
2. Divide the shredded chicken into six equal amounts and place in the papers.
3. Pour the broth equally over the chicken. Fill the papers with water until full (diluting the broth).
4. Put in the freezer.
5. Give the puppy one frozen chicken cube at a time, outside or on washable floors as the broth may stain carpet.

Rottweiler, 14 weeks old

Rottweiler, 15 weeks old

Trimming Toenails

You need to trim your puppy's toenails regularly. When nails grow too long, they can catch on things and break or rip. If the nail breaks below the quick, it will bleed and it's very painful.

Three types of nail trimmers are available. One is much like a pair of scissors with curved blades and another is called a *guillotine trimmer* and has a moving blade. The third is an attachment that fits on a rotary grinder. All three types work well, although the scissors type is probably easier for most new puppy owners to master.

Your puppy's nail grows just like yours does, out from the nail bed. The quick, which contains the blood vessels, is dense and appears pink in a white nail. The dead part of the nail, the part that you can trim, appears white on a white nail with the pink quick visible inside. Black nails, however, are dense and you cannot see the quick through the nail. But the nail grows in a semicircle and the quick is flat underneath the nail, with the trimmable part of the nail forming a curve.

> "Should you hit the quick and make your puppy bleed, scrape a bar of bath soap across her nail."

To trim the nails, first invite your puppy up on your lap. Take one paw and gently spread her toes. Pull the hair back from the nail, and if her nails are long, gently trim off the curved part of the nail. If she has worn off the hooked or curved part, just take a tiny bit off the end of the nail so she gets used to the process. Give her a special treat after you trim each nail and praise her.

Should you hit the quick and make your puppy bleed, scrape a bar of bath soap across her nail and then hold her in your lap for a couple of minutes. The soap will fill the nail until a clot forms.

Vaccinations

It has been common practice for many years to give a puppy multiple vaccinations during puppyhood and then to give booster vaccines each year for the rest of the dog's life. The vaccinations are for diseases such as bordetella, coronavirus, distemper, parvovirus, rabies, and many other diseases that can potentially threaten your puppy's health.

However, recently dog owners and many veterinarians are questioning the need for so many vaccinations and the annual booster requirement. The questions arise from the fact that even with better healthcare for dogs, they aren't living longer and many health problems (such as allergies and cancer) are getting markedly worse.

In response, many experts suggest that vets give vaccinations to puppies for those diseases that can potentially kill the puppy—such as distemper and parvovirus—and then any diseases that are active in the region. (Later, if you and your dog are going to travel to an area with a health threat that your puppy is not vaccinated for, then your puppy can get that vaccine prior to your trip.)

Many veterinarians are also checking blood titers (antibody counts) prior to giving the adult dog a booster vaccine. Many dogs will retain antibodies from the original vaccination given in puppyhood for many years, some even for a lifetime. This means an annual booster is unnecessary for these dogs.

Vaccinations are important; your puppy needs them. However, too many vaccinations can be detrimental. Talk with your veterinarian about the vaccination schedule she feels will suit your puppy best. As you talk with her, ask questions and feel free to ask her to explain her reasoning.

Clumber Spaniel, 15 weeks old

Sheltie–Australian Shepherd mix, 14 weeks old

Spaying or Neutering Your Puppy

The vast majority of all female dogs should be spayed and the males neutered. There is no shortage of puppies; just take a look at the classified ads in your newspaper or on the Internet and take a drive down to your local shelter or humane society. There are far too many puppies who will never find a good, forever home.

In addition, being a responsible breeder is a lot of work. It takes studying to understand pedigrees and how genetics affect the puppies. The potential mother and father of the litter must also get health checks to make sure they will not pass health problems on to their offspring, which includes X-rays for hip and elbow dysplasia, eye exams, and more.

Spaying a female puppy prior to her first *season* (period or mating season) has several benefits. First of all, you won't have to deal with the fuss and mess of her season, which occurs between 6 and 8 months of age. Keep in mind, most female puppies don't understand the need to wear pads or diapers!

Spayed female dogs have a lower risk of mammary gland cancers, reproductive organ cancers, as well as other kinds of cancer. Spaying also decreases the incidences of female aggression.

Neutering a male prior to adolescence (6 to 8 months) decreases the risk of cancer as well as many of the behaviors associated with a sexually mature male. He will be less apt to try and escape from the yard, less likely to fight with other male dogs, and he won't be as driven to mount other dogs. Although many neutered males still lift their leg to urinate, they aren't as annoying about it as intact males.

When to Call the Veterinarian

Raising a puppy is a lot of fun, but it's still challenging. It's even worse if your puppy doesn't feel good. Knowing when to handle a health problem at home and when to call the veterinarian can help. Keep your vet's phone number handy. Post it on the refrigerator and program it into your cell phone.

Call your veterinarian for guidance when or if:

- Your puppy has had diarrhea for more than twenty-four hours.

- The diarrhea has blood or mucus in it.

- Your puppy is vomiting repeatedly.

- Your puppy is refusing to eat and has missed two meals.

- Your puppy has a rectal temperature higher than 102.5 degrees Fahrenheit.

Emergencies that require an immediate trip to the veterinarian's office are listed on page 275.

When you call your vet's office, he will ask you several questions. Make sure you know the answers before you call.

- What is the specific problem?

- What made you notice it?

- What are the symptoms?

- When did your puppy eat last and how much did she eat?

- Is your puppy drinking water? More or less than normal?

- How is your puppy's activity level? Is she sleeping a lot? Playing?

Tell your vet anything else that might help. Then follow the veterinarian's instructions.

Poodle mix, 8 weeks old

Boxer, 14 weeks old

Emergencies

Emergencies can be life-threatening, so how you handle them is very important. Before anything happens, put together a first-aid kit for your puppy and keep it in a convenient location. You may even want two kits: one in the house and one in the car. (Your veterinarian can give you some guidance as to what to keep in the kit.)

Make sure you know your veterinarian's emergency procedures, too. During the day you can probably call the office and then rush your puppy in, but what happens after-hours? Call your vet and find out now so you know before something happens.

Some problems that constitute an emergency include:

- Bleeding that doesn't stop with direct pressure
- Wounds that gape open
- A snakebite of any kind
- A spider bite or a bee sting
- A bite by any wild animal
- Breathing difficulties, including gasping, wheezing, choking, or labored breathing
- Any eye injury
- Any suspected poisoning
- The ingestion of a foreign object
- Any potential allergic reaction, especially with swelling, red skin, welts, wheezing, or other reaction
- Lack of consciousness
- A broken bone

Call your vet right away and follow her instructions to the letter.

> **"Put together a first-aid kit for your puppy and keep it in a convenient location."**

Australian Cattle Dog, 12 weeks old

Chapter 11

As Your Puppy Grows Up

What Is Adolescence?

For better or for worse, puppies do grow up. But before your puppy becomes an adult, he's going to go through the adolescent stage, which will test the bond you have with him. As he matures, you can do so much more with him, like dog sports. His training should continue into adulthood, so consider enrolling him in advanced obedience classes, too.

Adolescence in dogs is the stage of life between puppyhood and adulthood. In dogs, adolescence can hit as early as 6 months of age and can last until 14 to 18 months of age. However, the worst of this stage is usually between 9 and 12 months old.

In puppyhood, puppies have instincts that urge them to follow adults. In a natural situation, where the puppies remain with their mother and do not go on to new homes, these are the adult dogs in their lives. Following the adult dogs helps the puppies learn how to function in the world and protects them from danger. When puppies live with people, this instinct tells the puppies to follow adult people for the same reasons.

However, by 6 to 9 months of age, the puppy is braver, more adventurous, far less compliant, and a lot more foolhardy! He wants to venture off on his own to explore, he's not as happy to follow adults, and he wants to think for himself.

You need to remember that this is a natural stage of development; your puppy has not turned into a bad dog. Nor is your puppy doing this to you because he's angry, or mad, or disgruntled. This is simply a part of growing up.

People turn far too many dogs into local shelters during this time period because they don't understand what is happening with their puppies. But you and your puppy can survive this stage.

German Shepherd Dogs, 14 weeks old

Australian Shepherd, 20 weeks old

Surviving Adolescence

When puppies turn into adolescents, people have a tendency to want to blame someone or something for the change in their puppies' behavior. They blame themselves by saying, "I chose the wrong puppy (or breed)" or, "I didn't spend enough time with the puppy." Or they blame the puppy, the breeder, or the dog trainer. None of these accusations has anything to do with adolescence.

There are several things you can do to survive your puppy's adolescence and keep your relationship with your dog intact.

- *Keep repeating to yourself, "It's not personal!"* Your puppy is not doing this to you.

- *A tired puppy is a happy puppy.* Kick up the exercise routine; he'll get into less trouble if he's tired.

- *Keep training.* Yes, the adolescent will challenge you and make training tough at times, but keep doing it.

- *Enforce your household rules.* And yes, he'll challenge these rules, too, but enforce them.

- *Be consistent.* Show your puppy that you expect good behavior all the time.

- *Be a good parent.* When he's pushing you and challenging you, don't lose your temper, be patient and kind, and do not back down.

Most importantly, look toward the future. As I'm writing this book, my husband and I have a puppy, Archer, who is in the throes of adolescence. He is silly, he's challenging, and he would like us to think he's never heard the word *sit* before in his life. At the same time, he is adorable, affectionate, and very vulnerable. So we love him, give him guidelines to follow, and we make sure he understands those rules. And I can already see that he's going to be a wonderful dog when he grows up.

Continuing Your Puppy's Training

You began your puppy's training when he first joined your household. You started the learning process with housetraining, then you taught him not to bite you, and finally you taught him the household rules. Next you taught him the basic obedience commands to continue his training.

But that's not the extent of training; it should continue on into adulthood. Keep in mind, the dog breeds we have today (and mixtures of those breeds) were originally designed to work for us. Some were hunters, some herded livestock, and others chased away predators. They all had a job to do. Very few were bred as pets.

When a dog with working instincts is kept as a pet and is given no mental challenges, he becomes bored. A bored dog, especially an intelligent dog who doesn't have enough to do, is going to get into trouble. He may bark too much, he may try to escape from the yard, or he may decide to dismantle your underground sprinkler system. However, if you continue to train him, you will keep his mind busy.

> **66** When a dog with working instincts is kept as a pet and is given no mental challenges, he becomes bored. **99**

His training can become his job—his occupation. As he gets better at it, you will find that he'll take pride in his job. My 4-year-old Australian Shepherd, Bashir, brings in the newspapers every morning, even on Sunday when the papers are huge, bulky, and heavy. This is his job and he takes pride in it; he wants to do it even when it's difficult.

Make training fun for both of you. Laugh when you make a mistake; after all, it's not the end of the world. Let your dog act silly, too. When Bashir drops the newspaper and it comes apart, I laugh and encourage him to bring me the separate pieces. It's all good.

Mastiff mix, 24 weeks old

283

Labrador Retriever–wolf mix, 24 weeks old

Physical and Mental Changes

You will see a number of changes in your dog as he grows up. These changes will vary, of course, depending upon the characteristics he inherited from his parents. If you were able to see his mother and father, you will have some idea of what your puppy will become when he grows up, but even then, your puppy is a unique individual.

As your puppy grows up, you will see some physical changes to his body. Although these characteristics vary by breed, these changes generally happen with most dogs:

- The chest deepens and widens.
- The hips broaden.
- The puppy coat disappears and the dog gets his adult coat.
- The puppy teeth are gone and the adult teeth grow in.
- He is less clumsy and more coordinated.
- He has more stamina for work and play.

You will see some mental changes, too.

- He can concentrate better and for longer periods of time.
- He can make better decisions.
- He is more watchful and protective.
- He is more affectionate with you, and you'll feel the bond with him strengthen.

Puppies are wonderful; they are all anticipation. But adult dogs are true companions; they are our best friends.

Checking Out Dog Sports

People enjoy doing things with their dogs, whether they go for a walk every morning or play catch. So, naturally, a number of dog sports are now available that people and their dogs can participate in.

- **Agility.** This is a dog obstacle course. You and your dog can do it for fun or as a competitive sport.

- **Carting.** Your dog learns to pull a wagon in this sport. Years ago, several breeds pulled wagons as an occupation. Today, you can participate just for sport or to get your dog to help you around the yard.

- **Flying Disc or Frisbee.** Tossing a flying disc so your dog can catch it is great fun and wonderful exercise for your dog. It is also a competitive sport.

- **Herding.** In this sport, your dog moves and controls livestock, which is practical for owners with farm animals. Or do it just for fun or for competition.

- **Hunting and Field Trials.** Many dogs were bred to help put meat on the table. Today, many people still hunt for food, but this is also a competitive sport.

Explore different things to do with your dog. Take your dog hiking and let him wear a backpack to carry his own water. When your family goes camping, let your dog come along. Dogs enjoy RV camping, too. Many dogs travel very well and can stay in hotels, motels, and bed and breakfast places with no problems at all.

There are many other sports available. Just do some Internet research or talk to your local dog trainer and other dog owners. And then remember to have fun!

Australian Shepherd, 11 weeks old

Pit Bull Terrier, 13 weeks old

Canine Good Citizen

The American Kennel Club (AKC) instituted the Canine Good Citizen (CGC) program to promote good dog owners and great dogs. Far too often the only time you hear about dogs in the media is when something horrible happens. But far more good dog owners and great dogs are around than bad ones, and the AKC felt it was time to acknowledge them.

The CGC consists of several, specific exercises that you and your dog must perform together. All of the exercises relate to real-life skills. When your dog completes the exercises correctly, he is awarded the "Canine Good Citizen" title and can then wear a collar tag that proclaims this.

The exercises include the following:

- A friendly stranger will walk up and greet you, but not your dog. Your dog must remain under control and accept the stranger without showing any aggression or fearfulness.

- A friendly stranger will approach and this time greets both you and your dog.

- Your dog must have good basic obedience skills, including sit, down, stay, come, and walk nicely on a leash.

- Your dog must be able to handle, without fear or anger, distractions that include sounds, sights, and movement.

- Your dog needs to remain calm when you leave him with a friendly person and you go out of sight.

> " Far more good dog owners and great dogs are around than bad ones. "

To find a CGC test in your area, contact a local dog trainer or go to the American Kennel Club's Web site at www.akc.org.

Therapy Dogs Provide Affection

Therapy dogs are something special and so are their owners. Therapy dogs and their owners work as a team. After training and certification, they visit day-care centers, schools, special education classrooms, nursing homes, hospitals, and senior day-care facilities to provide love and laughter to people who need it.

Dogs of all sizes, breeds, and mixed breeds can become therapy dogs. However, these are some of the requirements:

- The dog likes people and is well socialized to people of all ages, sizes, ethnic groups, and sexes.

- The dog is under good control: no jumping on people; no pawing or scratching; and no biting, mouthing, or excessive licking.

- The dog is well trained and able to sit, down, stay, walk nicely on a leash, and come when called.

- The dog is good around any equipment that he might encounter, including wheelchairs, walkers, canes, crutches, machines that make noises, and rolling carts.

In addition, the dog can have no behavior problems that could interfere with this volunteer work. For example, he needs to behave well around other dogs, cats, miniature horses, and even rabbits as these animals do volunteer therapy work, too.

For more information, including therapy-dog training and certification information, contact your local dog trainer or do a Web search for therapy dog groups in your area.

Maltese, adult

Archer and Bashir

Enjoy Your Dog!

Dogs are my profession and my life. I have been training dogs for thirty years, teaching dog-training classes for over thirty years, and writing about dogs since the mid-1980s. But most importantly, I can't imagine living life without a dog by my side. As I write these words, Archer, our adolescent puppy, is curled up under my desk with his head on my feet. Bashir, my awesome 4-year-old dog, is on the carpet behind my desk chair. And Riker, our 9-year-old, is lying on the tile in the hallway just outside my office.

My dogs provide companionship, which is important for a freelance writer who works at home. They make sure I get outside each morning to walk them and that I go outside a few times a day to throw the ball. I have many friends that I would never have met if I didn't have dogs. My husband, our dogs, and I have participated in many dog sports, including agility, carting, conformation, flyball, Frisbee, herding, obedience, search and rescue, therapy dogs, tracking, and much more. My dogs make me laugh, too, and I know that's good for me! Dogs are a vital part of my life.

Let your dog become an important part of your life, too. Don't isolate him out in the backyard; instead, invite him into your home and your heart. Granted, at times this is hard, especially during puppyhood and adolescence as he will get into trouble. But turning him into a civilized being is well worth the effort.

Photo Credits

Introduction

Page 2: Rogue, 3-hour-old Border Collie
Photo by Mary Fish Arango

Chapter 1

Pages 4 and 5: Robin's puppies, 6-week-old Golden Retrievers
Photo by Pamela Blake

Page 6: Anne and puppy Sara, 2-week-old Pug
Photo by Linda Sue Purkey, Green Gables Pugs

Page 8: Ella, 9-day-old Jack Russell Terrier
Photo by Diana S. Stewart

Page 11: Rogue, 3-week-old Border Collie
Photo by Mary Fish Arango

Page 12: Satch, 6-week-old Border Collie
Photo by Mary Fish Arango

Page 15: Panzer and Missy, 4-week-old Rottweilers
Photo by Katy Silva

Page 16: Mojo and Bella Luna, 16-day-old Labrador Retrievers
Photo by Christine Rinaldi Photography

Page 19: Cubby, 7-week-old Rottweiler
Photo by Katy Silva

Page 20: Emily, 2-year-old, and Bella Luna, 9-week-old Golden Retrievers
Photo by Christine Rinaldi Photography

Page 23: Sadie, 10-week-old Shih Tzu
Photo by Sheri Wachtstetter

Page 24: Lucy, 7-week-old Miniature Dachshund–English Cocker Spaniel mix
Photo by Breanne D W Karanakolas

Page 27: Coco's puppies, 9-week-old Labrador Retrievers
Photo by Jerald S. Davitz

Page 28: MacDuff, 11-week-old West Highland White Terrier
Photo courtesy of Celtic Irish Pups (permission from Marie Larkin)

Page 31: Gaylee, 8-week-old Golden Retriever–Labrador Retriever mix
Photo by Jan Newman

Page 33: Gabriel, 8-week-old English Shepherd
Photo by Gary E. Bertolin

Page 35: MacDuff, 14-week-old West Highland White Terrier
Photo by William F. Loutrel

Chapter 2

Pages 36 and 37: Great Pyrenees
Photo by Jean Fogle

Page 39: Rogue, 5-week-old Border Collie, with friend
Photo by Mary Fish Arango

Page 40: Hillary, 3-year-old Labrador Retriever–Golden Retriever mix; and Jasmine, 8-week-old Labrador Retriever
Photo by Sheri Wachtstetter

Page 43: Satch, 15-month-old Border Collie; and Mico, 6-week-old Border Collie
Photo by Mary Fish Arango

Page 44: Freckles, 14-week-old Australian Shepherd
Photo by Sheri Wachtstetter

Page 46: Panzer, Missy, and Cubby, 7-week-old Rottweilers
Photo by Katy Silva

Page 49: Missy, 7-week-old Rottweiler
Photo by Katy Silva

Chapter 5

Chapter 6

Chapter 7

Chapter 8

Chapter 9

Index